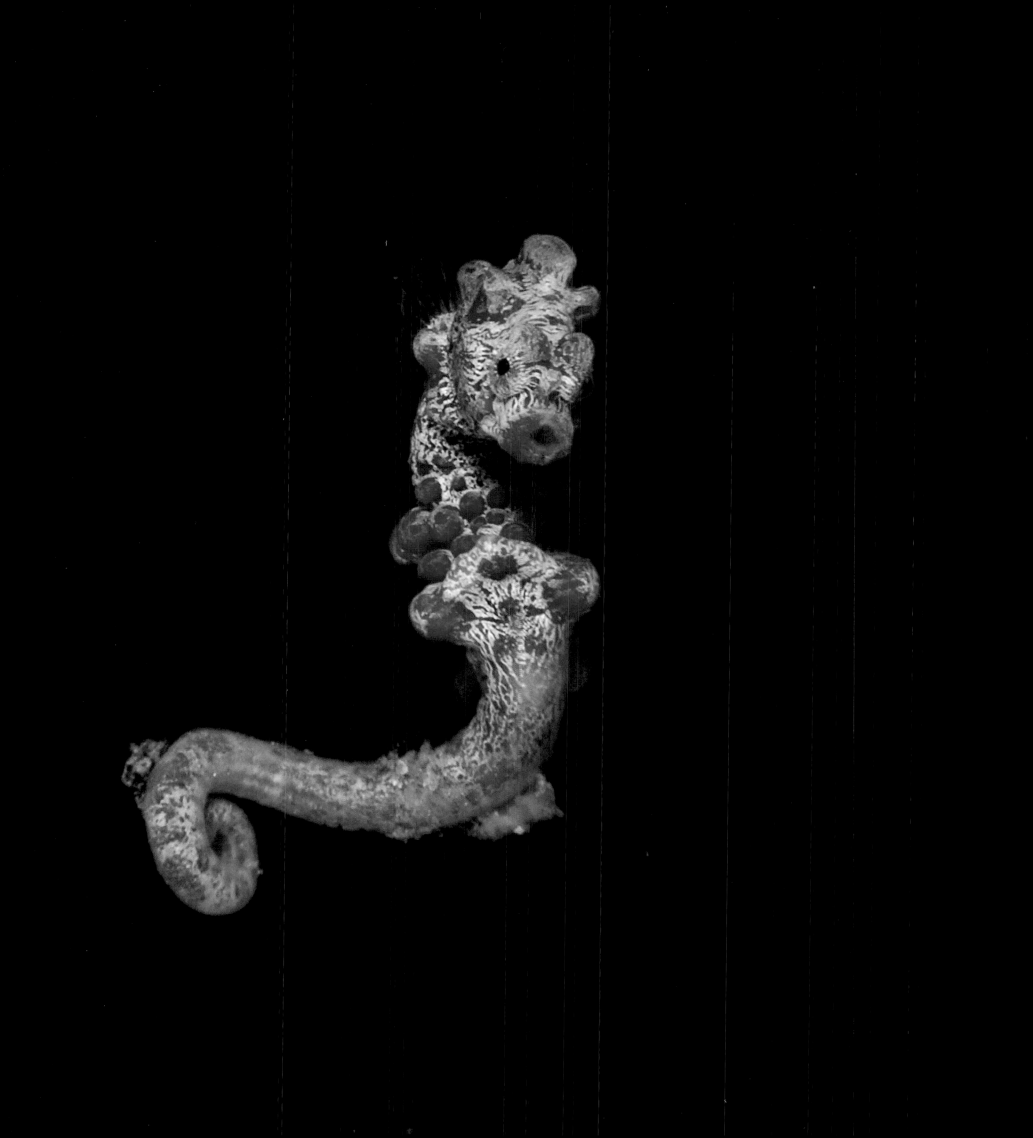

NATIONAL GEOGRAPHIC
WASHINGTON, D.C.

The Big BOOK of W.O.W.

CONTENTS

Prague Castle

Spirit bear

Holographic circus animals

Kraken

Australian ghostshark

Socotra dragon's blood tree

WOW! We enthusiastically say this word when something brings us great surprise or excitement.

International Space Station

It could be an animal whose size shocks us, a snapshot from space that stuns us, or a mystery from history that intrigues us. The universe is full of magnificent marvels that make our jaws drop, from the glittering expanse of the Milky Way galaxy to the colorful underwater oasis of the Great Barrier Reef.

Hang on tight as you gear up for a tremendous tour through the Wonders of Our World. You'll unveil the truth, the history, and the scientific explanations behind each one.

Get ready to dive in deep and search for the ocean's surreal surprises and meet the land's most captivating and curious creatures. Uncover awe-inspiring rarities—from unusual objects to uncommon occurrences to wild weather phenomena. And though Mother Nature knows how to make an impression, some of Earth's most mind-blowing sights aren't entirely natural. Many modern marvels are man-made, like radical roller coasters, sky-high swimming pools, and soaring skyscrapers.

Often, it takes unleashing your inner archaeologist to unearth some of the world's most lavish landmarks and tantalizing treasures. Ancient structures like the Great Pyramid at Giza and the Roman Colosseum offer glimpses to a world lost by time. But not all marvels are linked to the past—emerging technologies like flying cars and futuristic, eco-friendly cities are already taking us to new heights.

We're lucky to live in such a vast and surprising universe full of breathtaking beauty. As you flip through the pages of this book, become an adventurer and gaze at glistening galaxy formations, analyze ancient artifacts, encounter astounding animals, and investigate mind-blowing mysteries.

And always remember that with so many questions left unanswered and places left to explore, the delight of discovery still awaits with another "wow" in store.

Crooked House, Poland

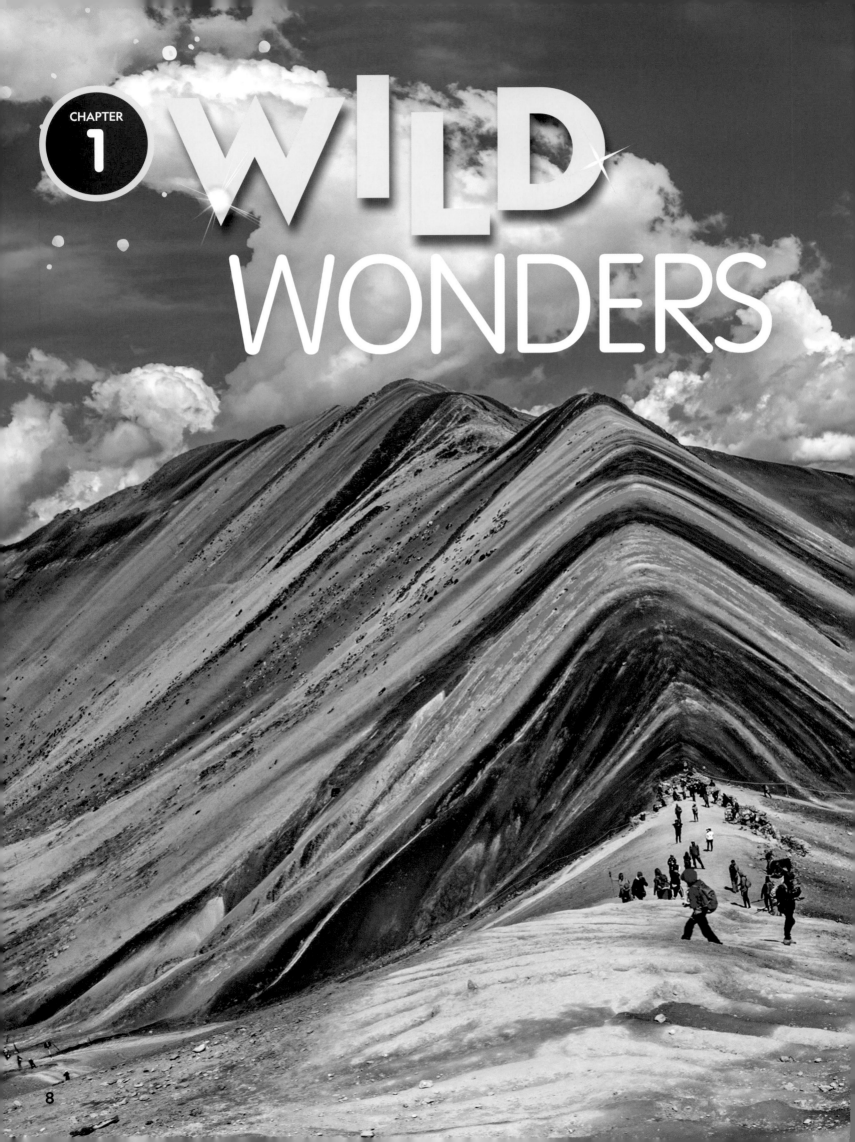

CHAPTER 1

WILD WONDERS

Mother Nature sure knows how to make an impression. In the great outdoors, you'll find all kinds of stunning natural wonders, from rainbow-colored rock formations to candy-scented plants to mega-strong storms. What's more, scientists continually discover new wonders in the wild! Get ready for a tour of some of the coolest spots and events on Earth.

Vinicunca mountain, Peru

TOP SEVEN NATURAL WONDERS

The world is chock-full of natural marvels. But seven have been named as the coolest, greatest, most gasp-worthy wonders on Earth. Find out which ones made the cut.

Victoria Falls

Where: On the border of Zimbabwe and Zambia

Whoooosh. That's a familiar sound at Victoria Falls, one of the largest waterfalls on Earth. This watery wonder, located on Africa's Zambezi River, rises as high as a 35-story skyscraper and stretches more than 15 American football fields in length. That huge size means a lot of H_2O. In fact, during the rainy season, enough water flows over the falls each hour to fill 1,635 Olympic-size swimming pools. And the splattering water creates so much mist, it's literally impossible to see the bottom of the falls. Talk about being endlessly cool!

Great Barrier Reef

Where: Australia

Dolphins dip and dive through the water. Sea turtles glide about looking for mates. Fish dart through swaying seaweed. The Great Barrier Reef, home to about 9,000 animal species, is like a bustling megacity for marine life. The reef might look like miles of colorful rocks, but it's actually made of teeny-tiny animals called corals. The reef formed over millions of years. First, young stony coral polyps clasped on to Australia's rocky eastern coast, absorbing minerals from the sea to help their skeletons grow. Then new corals repeatedly grew over the old coral skeletons, slowly making the reef even bigger. Today, it's so large that it can be seen from space.

Auroras

Where: North and South Poles

The night sky blazes with streaks of neon green, red, and purple. Is it a space party with huge strobe lights? Not quite. This phenomenon is called aurora borealis in the Northern Hemisphere and aurora australis in the Southern Hemisphere. It happens when the sun belches bubbles of charged gas, creating a solar storm that hurtles toward Earth. Our planet is protected by a magnetic field, but the field is weaker near the North and South Poles. So particles from the storm can enter our atmosphere and mingle with gases on Earth. The interaction generates colorful displays of light.

Mount Everest

Where: Spanning Nepal and Tibet

Mount Everest is a real rock star. It has earned worldwide fame for its incredible height. The tallest mountain on Earth above sea level, it soars 29,032 feet (8,849 m) in the air. That's 5.5 miles (more than 8.8 km), which is close to the cruising altitude of a passenger jet. And the peak keeps growing! Mount Everest first started to take shape between 50 and 60 million years ago, when two huge pieces of Earth's crust slowly crashed into each other and shoved land upward. That force is still at work, pushing the mountain about 0.2 inch (about 4 mm) higher each year.

Rio de Janeiro Harbor

Where: Brazil

This harbor boasts spectacular rock formations, more than 100 islands ... and an unsolved mystery. Also called Guanabara Bay, the nearly 20-mile (32-km)-wide site was carved out by the Atlantic Ocean over thousands of years. Portuguese sailors encountered the site in the 1500s. But they may not have been the first explorers to do so. In the 1980s, divers discovered what appeared to be ancient Roman artifacts in the bay. No one knows for sure how they got there.

Grand Canyon

This canyon lives up to its name. The 1,904-square-mile (4,931-sq-km) landform is larger than 11 million basketball courts. Up to 6,000 feet (1,829 m) deep, it could fit a stack of six Eiffel Towers at its deepest point. The canyon was sculpted over the course of six million years by river water flowing along its base. Today, it draws millions of tourists a year. But despite its popularity, the site still hides some secrets. Scientists recently found fossilized footprints in the canyon. They appear to belong to a strange reptile that wandered the area millions of years ago!

Parícutin Volcano

Where: Mexico

One February day in 1943, a cornfield in Mexico swelled and burst open. Lava and ash began shooting into the air. A volcano had unexpectedly come to life! The volcano continued erupting on and off for the next nine years. It grew bigger and bigger as more lava and ash settled and hardened. Then the formation suddenly went dormant. The volcano is still around today, towering 1,300 feet (400 m) high. It has been quiet for decades, but Parícutin's epic rise had a big impact: It allowed scientists to witness a volcano's birth for the first time ever.

HOW WERE THE WONDERS CHOSEN?

The news organization CNN compiled this list of the world's natural wonders in 1997. The list became a smash hit! Since then, other organizations have created their own roundups of nature's coolest marvels. But the CNN list continues to have staying power.

More
REMARKABLE ➤
ROCKS

➤ **ANTELOPE CANYON**
Where: Arizona, U.S.A.

➤ **MOUNT RORAIMA**
Where: Spanning Venezuela, Guyana, and Brazil

ONE **NATIONAL PARK** IN CHINA IS PACKED WITH **STONE PILLARS, MOST** MORE THAN TWICE THE HEIGHT OF THE **STATUE OF LIBERTY.**

HOW DID THIS LANDSCAPE TAKE SHAPE?

Zhangjiajie (jong-JIA-jeh) National Forest Park looks as if it belongs on a faraway planet. The park has more than 3,000 towering sandstone pillars topped with trees. And a dense fog often swirls around the pillars, making them seem even more alien.

But this region isn't part of an extraterrestrial landscape. It's in south-central China, and it took millions of years to form. The stone columns were sculpted by rainwater and ice. These elements slowly chipped away at the rocks like mini hammers and chisels. Plant roots that grew along the rocks also helped shape them. To highlight and preserve the scenery, in 1982 Chinese leaders turned the area into the country's first national park. Today, millions of visitors come each year to hike the land, catch a glimpse of the rhesus monkeys that hang out in the area, and, of course, gape at the park's spectacular stones.

EYE OF THE SAHARA
Where: Mauritania

SPLIT APPLE ROCK (TOKANGAWHĀ)
Where: New Zealand

HVÍTSERKUR SEA STACK
Where: Iceland

Extreme
EARTH

Where can you find the **WETTEST** place in the world? What about the **COLDEST** or the **STEEPEST**? Check out these **EXTREME DESTINATIONS** that test all the limits.

CRAZY CLIFF

Mount Thor keeps it steep. The peak, located in Canada, boasts the world's steepest cliff. It rises 4,101 feet (1,250 m) at an average angle of 105 degrees. The steepness results in a curving overhang that gives the mountain a hunched look.

LEVEL LAND

Salar de Uyuni in Bolivia is flat-out amazing—and also just really flat. In fact, this massive salt desert is the most level place on Earth. Salar de Uyuni is about as large as the state of Connecticut, U.S.A., yet its altitude varies by no more than three feet (1 m) throughout!

BRING ON THE *BRRRR*

Pack some extra-warm socks if you're heading to the East Antarctic Ice Sheet. This section of Antarctica is the coldest known place on Earth. Using satellite data, scientists determined that areas on the ice sheet's surface can drop to minus 144°F (-98°C)—as cold as night temperatures on Mars!

HOT SPOT

Summer temperatures in Death Valley, California, U.S.A., regularly top 120°F (49°C) ... in the shade! Why so hot? The valley is bordered by towering mountains that trap in heat. The scorching temperatures can make it difficult for wildlife to survive. But with just the right amount of rain and wind in springtime, wildflowers sprout across the valley in what's known as a "superbloom."

RIGHT AS RAIN

If there were awards for the wettest spot on Earth, Mawsynram, India, would be showered with prizes. This cluster of villages has the world's highest average rainfall, getting about 467 inches (1,186 cm) a year. To avoid getting soaked, out-and-about locals often wear full-body umbrellas made of bamboo and banana leaves.

DRY DESTINATION

The Atacama Desert in Chile is one of the driest spots on Earth. This arid destination can go years without a drop of rain. And in some parts of the desert, precipitation has *never* been recorded!

Mawsynram gets about 12 times more rain than Seattle, Washington, U.S.A.

Geyser BONANZA

WATCHING A GEYSER SPEW GALLONS OF WATER IS A REAL BLAST! Here's how geysers work: Rain and snow water seep into tubelike openings in the ground. Sizzling-hot magma sits inside these tubes. When the water gets close to the magma, it heats to a boil, and some water is forced back up. The boiling water creates steam. The steam pushes the water above it through the tube and into the air.

Fewer than **1,000 geysers** are active around the world.

There are **2** **types** of geysers: fountain geysers and cone geysers.

Earth's geysers occur in only **5 countries:** Chile, Iceland, New Zealand, Russia, and the United States.

Scientists detected more than **50,000 single eruptions** at Iceland's Strokkur geyser **in just one year.**

Wai-O-Tapu's Lady Knox Geyser, in New Zealand, erupts every day at **10:15** a.m.

Strokkur geyser, Iceland

Iceland's Great Geysir has been active for **around 10,000 years.**

At some geyser vents, water temperatures can be higher than **200°F** (93°C).

Pōhutu Geyser in Rotorua, New Zealand, can erupt **20 times a day.**

Yellowstone National Park, in the United States, features **two-thirds** of the world's geysers.

The Steamboat Geyser at Yellowstone shoots water **more than 300 feet** (90 m) **in the air.**

Some geysers can blast out more than **8,000 gallons** (30,283 L) **of water** during one eruption.

During the **first 20 or so seconds** of an eruption, water can shoot out of geyser vents at **1,125 feet a second** (343 m/s)— that's the speed of sound!

7 JAW-DROPPING **FACTS** ABOUT ...

PECULIAR PLANTS

You can't beat **EARTH'S GREEN SCENE.** The planet is filled with **PLANTS, TREES,** and **FLOWERS** that are both **BEAUTIFUL** and **BIZARRE.**

The **ROSE OF JERICHO PLANT** survives extreme desert heat by **CURLING INTO A TIGHT BALL** for the dry season and uncurling for the wet season.

One flower native to Mexico gives off the **SCENT OF CHOCOLATE.**

A rare flower that's **SHAPED LIKE A PARROT** grows in some tropical forests in **ASIA.**

Some bamboo can **GROW AROUND 35 INCHES** (89 cm) **A DAY**—that's longer than a skateboard.

Snake's head fritillary flowers have a **CHECKERED PATTERN.**

NIGHT-BLOOMING cereus cacti bloom only **ONCE A YEAR,** and only after dark.

The **VICTORIA AMAZONICA** water lily is strong enough to support a **KID'S WEIGHT.**

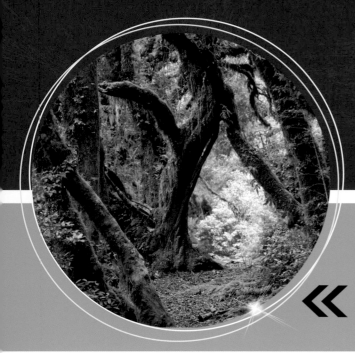

YILI VALLEY »

In spring, apricot blossoms burst open across China's Yili Valley. After the bloom, there's a bonus: The flowers bear juicy apricot fruit.

GOBLIN FOREST

After volcanic eruptions destroyed a New Zealand forest in about 1655, crooked trees sprouted from the fallen logs. Then hanging moss creeped over the twisty trunks and branches, giving the spot an enchanted feel. «

FAIRY-TALE

« NAMIBIAN SAND DUNES

Rising more than 1,000 feet (300 m), the sand dunes in Namibia's Namib Desert are the world's largest. They started to form some 80 million years ago with sand pushed by wind from the nearby coast.

SKAFTAFELL ICE CAVES »

The Skaftafell ice caves in Iceland get their blue hues from sunlight. Sunlight is made of multiple shades of color. As light filters into the caves through the ice, the frozen water absorbs most of these shades—except for blue.

PAINT MINES

The Paint Mines in Colorado, U.S.A., have orange-and-yellow rocks topped with white stones that resemble blobs of whipped cream. Erosion « carved these rocks from the ground, revealing layers of multicolored clay.

SPOTS

These places seem straight out of a storybook—but they're 100 percent real!

LAKE RETBA »

Lake Retba in Senegal has a ton of salt—10 times as much as ocean water! Algae that produce a reddish pigment thrive in this salty environment, turning the lake the color of bubble gum.

« PUNALU'U BEACH

This beach in Hawaii, U.S.A., gets its jet-black sand from lava that flowed into the ocean from a nearby volcano. The lava chilled in the cool sea and shattered into tiny grains. Waves push this black sand back to shore.

WONDERS
NEVER CEASE

Son Doong

Humans have been **exploring Earth** for thousands of years. So we must have long ago uncovered all of the world's **curiosities,** right? Wrong! Our planet continues to surprise us with its **marvels.** Here are some **amazing** more recent finds.

Son Doong

COLOSSAL CAVE

In 2009, a team of scientists descended into a mysterious cave covered by thick jungle in Vietnam. The entrance had been discovered in 1991 by a local logger. But the cave, named Son Doong, had yet to be explored. As the scientists clambered through the huge rocky chambers, they realized they might be stepping into the biggest known cave on Earth!

Later, the scientists used laser instruments to take precise measurements. It turned out that they were right—the cave is the largest on record, stretching more than five miles (8 km). Some parts are so big, a skyscraper could fit in them. Son Doong also has its own rainforest and river. The forest grew in one chamber after part of the ceiling collapsed, letting in rain, sunshine, and seeds. Even crazier? Small clouds often hang near the cave's ceiling, and the weather inside this enormous cave is often different from the weather outside. What a find!

FANTASTIC FALLS

Floods in 2010 devastated part of a forest in the Philippines. From the wreckage came a shocking discovery: Spectacular waterfalls had been hiding in the jungle. Villagers in the area were the first to encounter the hidden treasure. Two years later, a photographer won a nationwide contest with a picture of the falls. After that, the site became a hot spot for visitors.

The waterfall is called Asik-Asik in Hiligaynon, a native language of the region. Spanning 459 feet (140 m), Asik-Asik's water gushes from a plant-covered cliff. The source of

the waterfall may be an underground river or springs within the mountain. Though scientists still have a lot to learn about the site, it's already causing quite a splash.

ROCKY RAINBOW

Vinicunca isn't your average mountain. The Peruvian peak is decked out in subtle red, pink, blue, and yellow stripes. Experts think the mountain's coloring came from mineral deposits that built up over time and from weathering. With its busy, bright pattern, the peak really pops. So why didn't people notice it until around 2015?

Before then, the mountain was covered in ice. Climate change caused the snow and ice to melt, revealing the colors underneath. The mountain now faces an additional threat—tourism. In just a few years, the land has been damaged by an influx of visitors. Luckily, conservationists are working to guard this colorful peak.

VINICUNCA IS MADE UP OF 14 DIFFERENT COLORFUL MINERALS.

Vinicunca

AT NEARLY 200 FEET (60 M) HIGH, ASIK-ASIK STANDS TALLER THAN DISNEY WORLD'S CINDERELLA CASTLE.

Asik-Asik

SOUPED-UP

A supercell is a type of thunderstorm, only turbocharged. It appears as a massive pile of clouds—almost like a fluffy stack of pancakes! Fueled by a mighty column of rising air, it can spawn tornadoes, hail, and forceful wind gusts. Discover the secrets behind this power-packed storm.

These storms can hurl out HAIL THE SIZE OF GRAPEFRUITS.

➤ **LOCATION:**
Most common in the central United States

➤ **DURATION:**
Can last several hours

➤ **FREQUENCY:**
One in 1,000 thunderstorms becomes a supercell.

One out of every five or six supercells produces a TORNADO.

STORMS

Supercells can be more than 10 MILES (16 m) TALL (nearly twice the height of Mount Everest!) and around 12 MILES (19 km) ACROSS.

The rising air in the supercell, called UPDRAFTS, can move at 130 FEET A SECOND (40 m/s).

The storm's core is a tilted, tightly rotating tower of air called a MESOCYCLONE.

While regular thunderstorms form in clusters, a supercell is usually ISOLATED. That means it can suck up surrounding air for energy without having to "share" with other storms. This BOOSTS ITS HORSEPOWER.

Incredible
ISLANDS

You may actually want to **GET STRANDED IN THESE SPOTS!** Take a tour of amazing islands around the world.

For four months during the winter, the sun does not rise in Svalbard.

FROZEN WONDERLAND
Where: Svalbard, Norway

You'll feel on top of the world in Svalbard. This archipelago, or set of islands, is about 800 miles (1,200 km) from the North Pole. Svalbard, which is part of Norway, is packed with ice-covered mountains and glaciers. Yet it's considered a desert because it gets so little precipitation. Despite its harsh conditions, more than 2,000 people call Svalbard home. And they're not the only ones— polar bears outnumber humans on these icy islands!

EYE-POPPING PLANTS
Where: Socotra, Yemen

Saying Socotra is unique is an understatement. This island sits off the coast of Yemen. A third of its plants are found nowhere else on Earth. Socotra features dragon's blood trees, which look like giant pieces of broccoli and ooze red sap. It also has Socotra desert rose trees, which collect moisture and swell into the shape of bottles. What's more, one-of-a-kind animals like the Socotran chameleon live here. Now, that's a range of strange!

DOLPHIN-SHAPED ISLE
Where: Gallo Lungo, Italy

Gallo Lungo, which lies off Italy's southwestern coast, looks like a leaping dolphin. The adorably shaped island has a dramatic past. Ancient Greeks believed it held sirens, mythical creatures that bewitched sailors, making them crash their ships. Although these creatures weren't real, rough currents around the island did cause shipwrecks. Today, the Gallo Lungo is privately owned.

LOW LANDS
Where: Maldives

The Maldives is a chain of nearly 1,200 coral islands located in the Indian Ocean. Many of the islands rise no more than six feet (2 m) above sea level, making the Maldives the country with the lowest elevation on Earth. In addition to colorful coral reefs, the Maldives has majestic wildlife such as manta rays and whale sharks. This low-lying land will put you in high spirits!

GLITTERING BEACHES
Where: Matsu Islands, Taiwan

The Matsu Islands off Taiwan put on quite a light show. The water surrounding them can glow blue at night! The secret behind this phenomenon lies in balloon-shaped bioluminescent microorganisms in the water. These tiny living things, nicknamed sea sparkles, light up when disturbed by swimmers, waves, and boats. Unfortunately, too many of these "blue tears," as they're also called, can take oxygen from the water and produce toxic conditions for marine life. So this beautiful glow has a dark side.

Which Wonder WOULD YOU CHOOSE?
CROOKED FOREST vs.
SAGANO BAMBOO FOREST

Read about two spectacular forests and decide which one you'd most like to visit.

The trees in the Crooked Forest can grow 50 feet (15 m) tall.

Trees that surround the Crooked Forest grow straight up, with no curves.

People planted the forest around 1930, then fled the area around the start of World War II in 1939.

CROOKED FOREST
Where: Poland

This decades-old forest has an odd twist: Its 400 or so pine trees have curved trunks! The trunks grow horizontally along the ground before bending in an arc and shooting upward. How did the trees get their snakelike shape? Some people think they were damaged as young saplings, bent under the weight of heavy snow. Others think farmers tried to shape their growth into a crooked form, hoping to use the winding wood to make ships and furniture. In the years after the trees were planted, people living near the forest abandoned the area. They took their knowledge of what happened to the forest with them. These trees may forever remain a mind-bending mystery.

SAGANO BAMBOO FOREST
Where: Japan

Sagano Bamboo Forest is a delight for the eyes and the ears. Located outside the city of Kyoto, these woods are packed with thousands of towering bamboo stalks. And when wind blows through the bamboo, it creates a symphony of sound. The air hums as it sweeps around the plants. The stalks creak and click as they bend and knock together. And the leaves rustle in the breeze. With its natural beauty and calming sounds, Sagano Bamboo Forest has been a tourist magnet for hundreds of years. Guess people really want to see what all the noise is about!

A 14th-century Buddhist temple sits on the edge of the forest.

A troupe of Japanese macaques lives in a protected park near this site.

Bamboo has a greater tensile strength, or resistance to being pulled apart, than steel.

Sagano Bamboo Forest is often highlighted as one of the most beautiful forests in the world.

CHAPTER 2

ASTOUN
ANIMALS

Toco toucan

DING

They come in a rainbow of colors. Some are ultra flashy; others are masters of disguise. They can be the length of an airplane or too tiny for a human to see. Some boast superhero-like skills, and a few have some pretty cool dance moves! Earth's animals are living, breathing wonders. And when it comes to these critters, there's no stop to the surprises.

SEAHORSE SURPRISE

Brightly colored coral sits motionless underwater. Suddenly, a small piece wiggles back and forth. Wait, that's not part of the coral—it's a pygmy seahorse! This critter is the ultimate trickster. It grows to look so much like the coral it inhabits that you can barely tell the difference between them. Get the scoop on these camouflage champions.

As baby pygmy seahorses grow, they develop the exact same colors as the **CORAL** around them. How they do this is still a mystery.

Full-grown pygmy seahorses are at most only about an inch (2.5 cm) long, the diameter of a quarter. Their tiny size makes them vulnerable to predators, so using **CAMOUFLAGE** to hide in plain sight is a useful line of defense.

To match the coral's KNOBBY texture, the seahorse sprouts hard bumps known as TUBERCLES.

As babies, pygmy seahorses venture from their birthplace to find their own home. Once they settle on their chosen CORAL HABITAT, they spend the rest of their lives there.

Gripping the coral with its tiny tail steadies the seahorse. By LIMITING ITS MOVEMENT, the creature can blend in even more with its surroundings.

Pygmy seahorses can SWIM UP TO 500 BODY LENGTHS a second. (Compare that to cheetahs, which run 30 body lengths a second at full speed!)

Extinct
MARVELS

Some of Earth's **COOLEST CREATURES** went **EXTINCT** millions of years ago. But these long-gone animals certainly haven't been forgotten. Meet some of the most **SPECTACULAR** ones.

MEGA MYSTERY

Stegosaurus, the largest plate-backed plant-eating dinosaur, has long stumped scientists. It was once thought to have walked on two legs when it roamed Earth 145 million years ago. And scientists initially believed the bundle of nerves near its tail was a second brain. The purpose of the dino's plates isn't certain, though it's possible they were used to cool or warm the animal or to attract mates. And its spiked tail may have served as a weapon during fights. One thing's certain—*Stegosaurus* is a puzzle!

SOARING REPTILES

In prehistoric times, flying reptiles called pterosaurs (TER-uh-sores) ruled the skies. The *Alanqa* (Ah-LAN-kah) was one such creature. Living 100 million years ago, this pterosaur could weigh in at 200 pounds (90 kg) and sported a 20-foot (6-m)-long wingspan. That's about the length of two surfboards. The *Alanqa* had a spear-shaped, toothless jaw, which it might have used to pluck fish out of rivers or to snatch small baby dinosaurs off the ground. That's one ferocious flier!

TOP CROC

Aegisuchus (EH-jih-SOO-cus) was an ancient crocodile. It stretched 30 feet (9 m) and weighed some 20,000 pounds (9,000 kg). Its skull's shield-like shape earned the predator a cool nickname: ShieldCroc. Scientists believe the nearly 100-million-year-old crocodile may have used its unique head to fight off its enemies and regulate its internal temperature. To nab a meal, an *Aegisuchus* would wait in a river for large fish to swim by, then quickly snatch them up with its large jaws.

GO FISH

Baryonyx (BARE-ee-ON-icks), whose name means "heavy claw," existed 125 million years ago. The creature was named for its unusual thumb claw, which was more than a foot (0.3 m) long and possibly used to spear fish from rivers. What's more, the dino had long, narrow jaws studded with 100 teeth—twice as many as a *Tyrannosaurus*. With its claws and jaws, it's no wonder this dino draws oohs and aahs.

SNAZZY SKULL

Kosmoceratops (COZ-mo-SERR-uh-tops), which lived 76 million years ago, had a head topped with 15 horns. Little horns sat above the dino's eyes, and 10 hooklike bones poked out from the rear edge of its frill. Luckily, the creature had a big head to fit all these horns. At more than six feet (1.8 m) long, *Kosmoceratops*'s noggin was nearly as big as *Triceratops*'s, even though *Kosmoceratops* was only half the size!

SPIRIT BEARS ARE BLACK BEARS WITH COMPLETELY WHITE FUR.

WHAT'S THE SECRET BEHIND THE ANIMAL'S COLORING?

A streak of white flashes through a misty forest. It almost looks like a ghost that's haunting the woods. But this isn't a supernatural being—it's a white-colored black bear. That's right, black bears can sport white fur! These animals, often called spirit bears, get their rare coloring from their genes.

Genes are passed down from parents to offspring. They contain genetic codes that determine traits such as height, eye color, and hair color. Many black bear parents only carry genes for black fur, some only carry genes for white fur, and still others carry both. If a black bear receives a copy of the white hair gene from each of its parents, it will be covered in white fur. This doesn't happen very often, which is one reason these unique animals are so striking. They may not be ghosts, but spirit bears are sure to give you goose bumps!

Other GHOSTLY > CRITTERS

AUSTRALIAN GHOSTSHARK
This phantomlike fish has been haunting the sea for 400 million years. It swims in mild waters along continental shelves.

Most **SPIRIT BEARS** live in one spot: Great Bear Rainforest in British Columbia, Canada.

Spirit bears are also called **KERMODE** bears.

BARREL JELLYFISH

These spook-tacular jellies have eight frilly tentacles and travel in swarms of more than 100 individuals.

SNOW LEOPARD

This cat has almost supernatural moves: It can leap 30 feet (9 m), or six times its body length!

7 JAW-DROPPING **FACTS** ABOUT …

ANIMAL
HABITS

Some creatures really **CRANK UP** the weird factor. Check out some **TRULY STRANGE** animal behaviors.

The **WESTERN SPOTTED SKUNK** sometimes does a **HANDSTAND** before spraying foes. ▼

A type of **LEMUR** called the **SIFAKA** moves across the ground by doing a **SIDEWAYS HOP.**

Hungry archerfish **SPIT WATER AT INSECTS** to knock them from plants **INTO THE WATER.** ▼

BELUGA WHALES blow different types of **BUBBLES** depending on **THEIR MOOD.**

◄ Horned lizards **SQUIRT BLOOD** from their **EYES** to scare enemies.

Female ruby-throated hummingbirds **"GLUE" TOGETHER THEIR NESTS** with **SPIDER SILK.** ▼

Waxy monkey tree frogs **OOZE A WAXY SUBSTANCE** and then **RUB IT ON** their bodies as **SUNBLOCK.**

CHRISTMAS TREE WORM »

Christmas tree worms, which measure about 1.5 inches (4 cm) and live underwater, have tube-shaped bodies with extensions that resemble fir trees. The "trees" are made of hairlike bristles, which are used for breathing and for catching small, yummy plants that float by.

« SEA BUTTERFLY

The 0.4-inch (1-cm)-long sea butterfly, a type of sea snail, isn't a slow mover. It swims by fluttering its winglike foot flaps, looking as if it's flying underwater.

MICRO-

« HAIRY SQUAT LOBSTER

Hairy squat lobsters— a type of crab—dazzle with their pink and purple hues. What's more, their bright, 0.6-inch (1.5-cm)-long bodies are covered in luxurious white hairs. The animals use the hairs to collect snacks to eat later.

RED VELVET MITE >>

About the size of a small raisin, the red velvet mite is pretty cute. But this critter has a not-so-sweet surprise for predators—it tastes awful! The mite's red color warns foes about its gag-worthy flavor.

GLOBULAR SPRINGTAIL

You could call this animal a little jumpy. No bigger than a pencil point, the critter has a tail-like body part tucked under its belly. When disturbed, it uses the tail as a spring, catapulting itself away from danger. <<

CRITTERS

Welcome to the wondrous world of teeny-tiny animals.

PEA APHID ∧

The pinhead-size pea aphid is one high-energy animal—literally! Scientists think the itty-bitty insect can capture sunlight and transform it into energy, in a way similar to how a plant does it. No other animal on Earth has been known to do this.

<< WATER BEAR

They may be microscopic, but water bears (also called tardigrades) are one of the hardiest animals on Earth. They can survive for decades without food or water, withstand extreme temperatures, and even endure a trip to outer space.

Which Wonder WOULD YOU CHOOSE?
ANIMAL SUPERPOWER SHOWDOWN

If you had to choose just one, which amazing animal ability would you pick? Read on, then select your superpower.

This feline has the longest legs for its body size of any cat.

Servals use their long limbs to scoop fish out of water.

Reindeer are also called caribou in North America.

The reindeer has a special nose that warms air before it reaches the lungs.

JUMPING POWER

Talk about having a bounce in your step. The serval, a wild cat native to parts of Africa, is an amazing jumper. It can leap 10 feet (3 m) straight up from a standing position—that's about twice the height the best human athletes could jump from the same position! Servals use their legendary leap to hunt, springing up and grabbing birds right out of the air with their jaws! The serval's jumping skills really pay off, helping it become the most successful hunter of all the cats in Africa. If you could perform these leaps, think how far you'd go!

SUPER VISION

During winter, reindeer living in the frigid Arctic must deal with months of darkness. These animals don't exactly have flashlights lying around. So how do they see? A type of light called ultraviolet (or UV) light still scatters over the region. When it hits Earth's surface, it reflects off of the snow. UV light is invisible to humans, but a reindeer's eyes are so sensitive that they can pick up on it. With this light, reindeer can see enough to get a sense of their surroundings. It's almost like having built-in night-vision goggles. Who wouldn't want a pair of those?

Depending on the species, pufferfish range from one inch (2.5 cm) to up to three feet (0.9 m) long.

Pufferfish produce a powerful toxin that they also use to fend off enemies.

SHAPE-SHIFTING

A small pufferfish spots a shark rushing toward it. What's the vulnerable marine animal to do? Go into Hulk mode, of course! The pufferfish has an elastic stomach that can easily expand. When threatened, the fish gulps water into its belly, causing its body to swell. In no time, it can more than double in size, making it harder for predators to snag the fish. Their ability to go big is pretty eye-popping and essential to their survival. Is shape-shifting the power for you, too?

Whale of an ANIMAL

BLUE WHALES ARE A BIG DEAL—EMPHASIS ON BIG. One blue whale can stretch 100 feet (30 m). That's the length of a commercial jet! In fact, these creatures are the largest animals to ever exist, even bigger than the largest known dinosaurs. But this whale's massive measurements are just one of its amazing stats. Check out the numbers on these jumbo-size marine mammals.

In areas with lots of food, groups of up to **60 blue whales** may gather.

Blue whales can live **80** to **90** years.

Adult blue whales can weigh around **300,000 pounds** (136,000 kg)—more than three semitrailer trucks.

They can swim more than **20 miles an hour** (32 km/h) for short bursts.

A blue whale's spout can rise **30 feet** (9 m) into the air—that's the height of a three-story building.

They can dive up to **1,640 feet** (500 m) below the sea's surface.

Baby blue whales gain nearly **200 pounds** (91 kg) a day.

Instead of teeth, blue whales have **300 to 400 baleens**—fringed brushes through which they filter food.

A blue whale's heart beats **11 times** a minute; a human's beats up to 90 times a minute.

The whale's songs can travel more than **600 miles** (1,000 km) underwater.

More
SPECTACULAR
SPIDERS

CHECK OUT THESE
AMAZING ARACHNIDS.

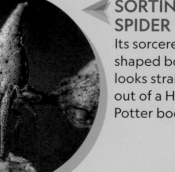

SORTING HAT SPIDER
Its sorcerer-hat-shaped body looks straight out of a Harry Potter book!

PEACOCK SPIDERS PERFORM ELABORATE DANCES FOR ONE ANOTHER.

WHY DO THESE ARACHNIDS BOOGIE?

Cue the music. When male peacock spiders spot potential mates, they get their groove on. To wow females, the arachnids vibrate, strut back and forth while showing off a bright abdominal flap, and wave their legs in the air. Not only do these spiders have all the moves—their backsides are also decked out in a rainbow of colors, making the performance even flashier. Even so, the females can be tough critics. If they don't like the dance, they might shake their stomachs at the males. If they *really* don't like it, they might gobble up the performers!

Even if the females aren't always impressed, scientists are. According to experts, the peacock spider's mating dance is one of the most extravagant in the animal kingdom. You might need a magnifying glass to see it, though. The arachnids, which are native to Australia, are so small they'd fit on your fingertip! They prove that even tiny critters can put on a big show.

SPINY ORB-WEAVER
The spider's small spikes warn enemies to stay away.

GREEN LYNX SPIDER
It jumps up and catches yummy insects in midair.

BRAZILIAN CRAB SPIDER
This critter resembles flowers to trick prey.

TOCO TOUCAN

This toucan uses its orange beak to control its body temperature. If it's too hot, the bird sends blood rushing to its beak, where heat from the blood can escape. When cold, the bird keeps blood from flowing to the beak to limit heat loss.

JAVAN GREEN MAGPIE »

You are what you eat—just ask the Javan green magpie. The bird gets its lime green color from its diet of insects. The insects store a green pigment from the leafy plants they nibble on.

BRIGHT

SCARLET MACAW »

The scarlet macaw is bright and loud, but it has a soft side. This bird has one mate for life. It spends hours each day grooming its partner's feathers. And it even gives face licks to show affection. Aww!

ROSEATE SPOONBILL

« A hungry roseate spoonbill dunks its head in water and swings it from side to side. The bird's sensitive bill can feel movement from nearby animals. Once it senses prey, the bird snaps it up in its spoon-shaped bill. Dinner is served!

AMERICAN GOLDFINCH »

The American goldfinch deserves a gold medal for its nests. It makes them with plant fibers, weaving the fibers together so tightly that the nests could hold water like a cup! The bird even steals sticky spider silk to attach its nests to branches.

BIRDS

These fliers bring a splash of color to the animal kingdom.

BLUE-FOOTED BOOBY

Male blue-footed boobies flaunt their turquoise tootsies to attract mates. After having chicks, the birds use their feet for another purpose—covering their young to keep them warm. »

RAVEN

These birds are brainiacs. Ravens can imitate human voices and use their wings and beaks to point at things, just as humans do with their fingers. The birds even pretend to place food in one spot but hide it in another to fool potential food thieves. «

MEERKATS

MEERKATS ARE ALL ABOUT TOGETHER TIME. These critters, which are part of the mongoose family, live in packs called mobs. They spend their days working as a group to find food, care for babies, and guard territory. They even sleep in furry piles! Although meerkats often fight each other for dominance, they depend on one another to survive. Dig into fantastic facts about these fuzzballs.

Insects make up about **80 percent** of a meerkat's diet.

Meerkats make **more than 30 types of vocalizations,** from purrs to barks to whistles.

While meerkat families hunt, **at least 1 member** keeps a lookout for predators. This individual is known as a sentry. If it spots danger, the sentry squeals with a high-pitched warning.

A meerkat can spot a flying eagle from **more than 1,000 feet** (305 m) away.

A meerkat burrow, or underground shelter, can be **6.5 feet** (2 m) **deep** and have up to **90 entrances.**

According to some estimates, meerkats can tolerate **6 times the amount of snake venom** that would kill a rabbit.

Meerkats can run up to **20 miles an hour** (32 km/h).

Meerkat mobs can include **up to 40 individuals.**

Baby meerkats first open their eyes **2 weeks** after being born.

These animals spend about **5 to 8 hours a day** foraging for food.

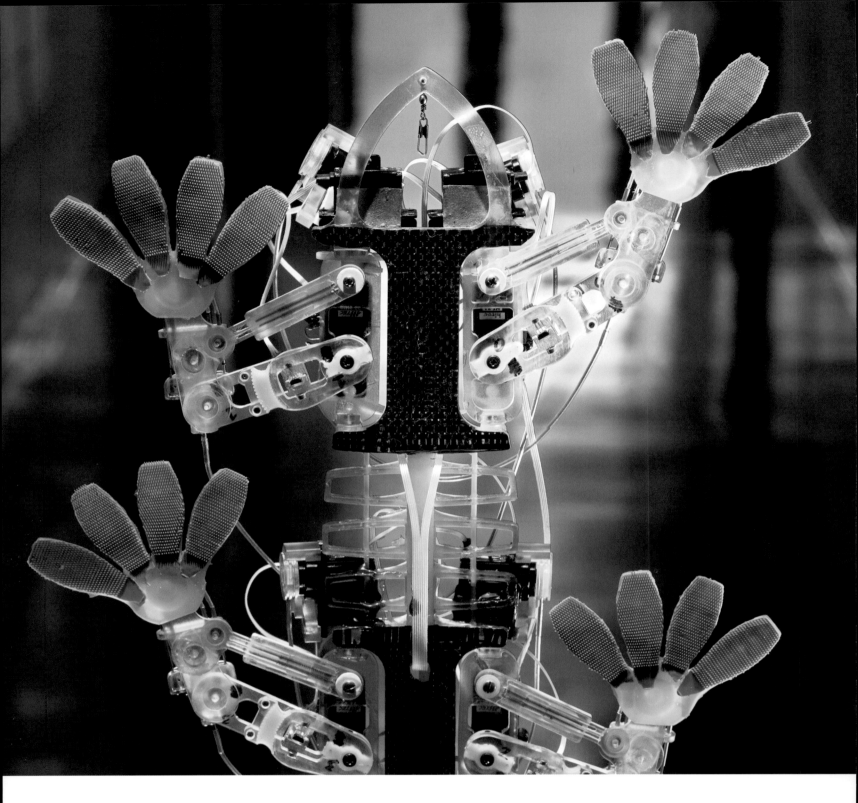

ROBO-REPTILE

Geckos have no shortage of fans. They've long been admired for their ability to **cling to smooth surfaces,** even while **hanging upside down.** But one group of scientists took their interest in the reptile to the next level: They created a **gecko-inspired robot** that can scale walls!

STICKY INSPIRATION

Roboticists at Stanford University in California, U.S.A., were looking to build a robot that could scoot up slippery structures. They didn't want to use suction cups in the design because those would slow the robot down. So they had to come up with another idea. Enter the gecko.

Geckos, which are found on every continent except Antarctica, are like animal stunt performers. They can zip up vertical surfaces, crawl across ceilings, and even dangle upside down by one toe! The secret to their gravity-defying moves lies in their feet. Gecko toe pads are covered in millions of tiny hairs called setae (SEE-tee). The hairs have a strong electromagnetic attraction to surfaces, providing cling power. The scientists at Stanford wanted to see if they could create a machine that could copy the gecko's sticky tricks.

READY, SET, CLIMB!

To make their gecko bot, the scientists designed a motorized mechanical frame shaped like the real reptile. They also designed a rubberlike material with tiny artificial hairs similar to a gecko's. The scientists attached this material to each of the robot's four feet. Then they set the robot to climbing mode and let it loose on the smooth walls of the lab. Sure enough, the bot was able to clamber up these surfaces!

The scientists had succeeded in creating a robo critter with gonzo gripping abilities. Their creation, known as Stickybot, was a great example of biomimicry: modeling inventions or products after animals or plants. But could the technology be useful outside the lab? Absolutely!

SAVING LIVES AND SERVING TAKEOUT

A hiker with an injured leg sits on a hard-to-reach ridge of a cliff. Suddenly, a buzzing sound fills the air. A small drone carrying medical supplies swoops into view. Outfitted with the clingy material made for Stickybot, the drone is able to attach itself to the cliff wall and deliver the supplies.

Drones with Stickybot parts that could aid in search-and-rescue missions are just one possible use of this robot. A gripping drone could also deliver takeout food in cities, sticking itself to the windows of tall buildings. Scientists have even experimented with using Stickybot material to make climbing gear for people. That means one day you could scale a wall just like a gecko. It's pretty clear—Stickybot has real sticking power!

IN ADDITION TO THEIR CLIMBING ABILITIES, GECKOS CAN MAKE AN IMPRESSIVE RANGE OF NOISES. THEY HISS, SQUEAK, CLICK, CROAK, AND BARK.

GECKOS CAN RUN ACROSS THE WATER'S SURFACE, MOVING THREE FEET PER SECOND (0.9 M/S).

BREATH BYGONES

TAKING

A lavish ancient city carved out of stone. Legendary landmarks said to bring luck and fortune to visitors. Long-standing castles hiding crazy-cool secrets. The world's age-old wonders have been making jaws drop for centuries—some even long after they've disappeared! And these historic gems give us amazing clues about how people lived in the past. Turn the page for the scoop on some spectacular old-school marvels.

Borobudur Temple, Indonesia

ANCIENT WONDERS OF THE WORLD

The seven wonders of the ancient world were designated in 250 B.C.—more than 2,000 years ago. Each of the structures were hailed as ingenious feats of engineering and sites of great beauty. Unfortunately, you can't jet off to see these marvels today—only one of the seven ancient wonders still exists!

Great Pyramid at Giza

Where: Egypt
Built: ca 2550 B.C.

This pyramid sparkled when it was first built more than 4,500 years ago. Though it appears brown now, the Great Pyramid at Giza was originally covered in a type of gleaming white limestone said to reflect the sun's radiant rays. The largest of a group of three pyramids commissioned as tombs for pharaohs, it was the tallest structure in the world for more than 4,000 years and is the only ancient wonder still standing today. Though many question how the Great Pyramid was built, experts believe it took a whopping 20,000 to 30,000 workers, more than two million extremely heavy stones, and 10 to 20 years to complete.

Hanging Gardens of Babylon

Where: Babylon (modern-day Iraq)
Built: ca 600 B.C.

Imagine entering a lush garden where multiple levels of white stone terraces tower above you, each housing exotic and vibrant plants, some of which look like they're float-ing. This beauty was said to have existed at the Hanging Gardens of Babylon. Word of its magnificence traveled fast, and even today, the garden is renowned for its massive size, unique engineering, and amazing water irrigation system. But with no surviving firsthand accounts from witnesses and little to no archaeological proof, scholars debate whether it ever truly existed!

Statue of Zeus at Olympia

Where: Greece
Built: ca 460–457 B.C. (temple), ca 430 B.C. (statue)

In Olympia, the famous site of the Olympic Games, stood a glorious temple honoring the father of all Greek gods: Zeus. Within the temple walls was an even more astounding sight: a 40-foot (12-m)-tall sparkling statue of Zeus himself sitting on a mighty throne—that's as tall as a four-story building! Zeus's statue was a feast for the eyes. His skin was carved from creamy ivory; his beard, robes, and staff were covered in glittering gold; and select pieces were adorned with expensive jewels. It stood for 1,000 years before it was ultimately destroyed by earthquakes in the sixth century A.D. So where did all that wealth end up? No one knows for sure!

Temple of Artemis at Ephesus

Where: Asia Minor (modern-day Turkey)
Built: ca 550 B.C.

In the sixth century B.C., a brilliant temple was built to honor Artemis, the Greek goddess of hunting, wild animals, forests, childbirth, and fertility. Reportedly designed by a master architect named Chersiphron, the temple left visitors in awe of its incredible size and immaculate details. According to ancient sources, the temple was nearly twice the size of the famous Parthenon in Athens, Greece, stretching longer than 425 feet (130 m) and reaching about six stories tall with a height of 60 feet (18 m). The marble temple, covered in intricate carvings and decorated with gold and silver, featured incredible pieces of art and statues within. Unfortunately, the wonder was destroyed and rebuilt multiple times before finally being torn down for the last time in A.D. 401, leaving only the foundation and one lonely column.

Mausoleum at Halicarnassus

Where: Turkey
Built: 350 B.C.

This towering square tomb was built for the ruler Mausolus, who was praised for transforming the coastal city of Caria into a desirable destination for important goods to flow through. He added many buildings, roads, and even helped neighboring cities. As someone who made such an incredible impact, an equally incredible burial structure to honor his legacy was in order. The massive mausoleum towered a few stories high and was adorned with gorgeous carvings, art, and columns made of marble. It was topped with a giant statue of Mausolus riding a chariot. This ancient wonder is one reason why we call large burial structures mausoleums to this day!

Colossus of Rhodes

Where: Greece
Built: 280 B.C.

With its five harbors, the ancient Greek city-state of Rhodes was an ideal location for trade. Because of this, many rulers tried to conquer the land for their own. One such ruler, King Demetrius of Macedonia, besieged the city in 305 B.C. for an entire year! But the people of Rhodes stood their ground, and Demetrius was finally forced to give up. In honor of this freedom and in the hopes of continued prosperity, the city commissioned a local sculptor named Chares of Lindos to build a gigantic statue made of brilliant bronze that gleamed in the sun. Named the Colossus, the statue depicted the Greek sun god, Helios.

Lighthouse of Alexandria

Where: Egypt
Built: 300–280 B.C.

The magnificent Lighthouse of Alexandria was built to steer ships safely to harbor—and to serve as a monument to Alexander the Great, the founder of Alexandria. At the top of the stone-and-silver lighthouse was a bronze mirror that reflected the sun during the day and a fire at night to prevent shipwrecks. The lighthouse toppled over in the A.D. 1330s. Many of the remains were removed, but pieces of the lighthouse were discovered underwater. Travelers from all over the world can scuba dive to view them.

7 NEW WONDERS

In 2007, the New 7 Wonders Foundation held a public vote to choose an updated set of seven wonders. Check out the "new" wonders!

 1 ### The Great Wall
Where: China
Built: 220 B.C.–A.D. 1644

 2 ### The Taj Mahal
Where: India
Built: A.D. 1632–1648

3 ### Petra
Where: Jordan
Built: ca 312 B.C.

MORE ABOUT PETRA ON PP. 62–63

 4 ### The Colosseum
Where: Italy
Built: A.D. 72–82

5 ### Christ the Redeemer
Where: Brazil
Built: A.D. 1926–1931

6 ### Chichen Itza
Where: Mexico
Built: ca A.D. 550

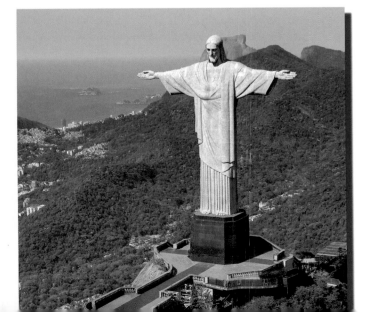

7 ### Machu Picchu
Where: Peru
Built: ca A.D. 1450

LOST AND FOUND

Journey through a narrow canyon gorge in the hills of Jordan and you'll discover Petra, a mysterious ancient city full of temples, tombs, and houses intricately carved into the red rock walls. More than 2,000 years old, this wondrous feat of astounding architecture features more than 800 structures. The city, lost to the known Western world for nearly 1,000 years, was rediscovered in 1812. Even now, only 15 percent of the city has been uncovered—tons of new archaeological discoveries await!

Petra is also called the Rose City due to the blushing pink-and-red color of rock.

The colorful rock is said to glow at sunset and sunrise.

The Treasury has two stories standing 128 feet (39 m) tall.

Several Greek scrolls were found in the Temple of the Winged Lions and are being studied in the hopes of shedding light on life in Petra.

The entire city spans more than 100 square miles (260 sq km).

The city's population reached about 30,000 people.

Petra was declared one of the seven new wonders of the world in 2007.

Scenes from the movie *Indiana Jones and the Last Crusade* were filmed in the area.

Petra included a grand theater that is thought to have seated 6,000 people.

More HIDDEN GEMS

▶ **ANGKOR WAT**
Where: Cambodia
Built: A.D. 1113–1150
Beautiful stone structures covered in lush moss give this hidden Buddhist temple an ethereal feel.

▶ **LESHAN GIANT BUDDHA**
Where: Sichuan Province, China
Built: A.D. 713–803
The largest carved stone Buddha statue in the world goes almost unnoticed due to the greenery that has taken over.

▶ **DERINKUYU**
Where: Cappadocia, Turkey
Built: ca 800–600 B.C.
One of the largest underground cities found in the region includes 18 underground stories and was capable of housing 20,000 people.

FANCY FROGS

The Coclé people, who thrived in present-day Panama more than 1,000 years ago, thought of frogs as weather forecasters. Their calls were believed to signal the start of the rainy season. This made frogs popular subjects in Coclé artwork and jewelry, like gold pendants.

JAGUARS IN CHARGE »

Jaguars are so athletic that the Maya believed they had superpowers. Fascinated by the cats' strength, Maya artists produced countless carvings of them; these were often made from jade, which was more valuable to the Maya than even gold. Only the best for these felines!

ANIMAL

« CAT WALK

The ancient city of Babylon (located in present-day Iraq) was known for its riches and beauty. And one of its roads had some truly fierce decorations: Walls lining the walkway were covered in glazed tiles featuring lions. These striking designs were meant to scare enemies.

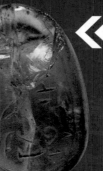

BEETLE BODYGUARD

Ancient Egyptians carved representations of the cherished scarab beetle out of gems like amethyst to create good-luck charms, or amulets. These were not only used by the living—they were also placed within mummy wrappings to keep the mummies safe in the afterlife.

CAVE CREATURE

The Altamira cave system in Spain is home to a very old herd of bison—sort of! It's filled with 20,000-year-old paintings of the animals. To make the paint, cave artists ground colored rocks into powder, then turned this into paste with spit or water. They used their fingers or twigs to leave their mark.

ARTWORK

From jade jaguars to ceramic owls, art from the past has a serious wild side.

OWL ARTWORK

In ancient Greece, owls were serious VIPs. The birds, which were revered for their ability to see in the dark, became a symbol for Athena, the Greek goddess of wisdom. To honor these animals, people painted them on vases, bowls, and other ceramics.

BUTTERFLY BONANZA

Hundreds of years ago in China, butterflies—considered a symbol of long-lasting life in art—fluttered their way onto paintings, porcelain, and silk garments. This butterfly-clad robe from the 19th century may have been worn at celebrations to bring people joy and good fortune.

MYSTERY
of ATLANTIS

According to an ancient legend, Atlantis was an island **paradise** complete with **posh palaces,** glittering harbors, and groves of juicy fruit. Then, in a single day, **it vanished.** It's a captivating story—but is it true? Read on and **decide for yourself.**

MISSING CITY

The story of Atlantis first appeared around 360 B.C. in the writings of Plato, an ancient Greek philosopher. As Plato tells it, Atlantis was a swanky empire covered with lush gardens and grand palaces. Wild animals such as elephants roamed the leafy land, and fruit trees provided enough eats for nightly feasts. Plato wrote that the civilization thrived for many years, until sudden, violent earthquakes whipped up giant waves that drowned the island. Within a day, it disappeared.

For thousands of years, people have wondered if Plato's story was real. If Atlantis did exist, then a pile of valuable artifacts could be stashed where the island sank. Using cutting-edge technology and Plato's writings as a guide, curious adventurers have struck out to try to locate the lost island.

LOOKING FOR CLUES

After infrared satellite imagery revealed what looked like buildings buried beneath mudflats in Spain, historian Richard Freund traveled to the area. He believed Atlantis may have been located there before being drowned by a tsunami and then covered in mud deposits. Freund's team shot electric currents into the ground. By examining how the currents moved, they could detect objects up to 40 feet (12 m) deep. Results showed that there was something deep inside the mud—perhaps a disintegrated wall.

Freund's theory isn't the only one. Explorer Robert Sarmast believed that quakes and volcanic eruptions wrecked the city. He took images of a submerged island in the Mediterranean Sea that supposedly show evidence of canals and walls matching Plato's description. Some have even suggested that Atlantis lies under a polar ice cap!

CASE CLOSED?

Although several people have tried to unearth the secrets of Atlantis, most scientists think the island is completely fictional. Some point out that no one—not even the researchers with cool findings—has dug up solid proof that Atlantis existed. Others mention that Plato's story was set in the Stone Age, long before a sophisticated city like Atlantis could have existed.

According to Plato, the natural disasters that destroyed Atlantis were sent by gods infuriated with citizens for being selfish. This has led many to conclude that the story was created as a fable to remind people to be less greedy.

Whether or not you believe the story of Atlantis is real, one thing's certain: This age-old mystery may be unsinkable.

Illustration of Plato

PLATO, WHO LIVED FROM AROUND 428 B.C. TO 348 B.C., WROTE MORE THAN 35 DIFFERENT WORKS. ATLANTIS IS MENTIONED IN TWO OF THEM.

ACCORDING TO PLATO, THE KINGS WHO RULED ATLANTIS DESCENDED FROM POSEIDON, THE GREEK GOD OF THE SEA.

More FANCY ➤ WONDERS

➤ **IGLESIA DE LA COMPAÑÍA DE JESÚS**
Where: Quito, Ecuador
Built: A.D. 1605–1765
The church, which took 160 years to complete, houses walls covered in gold leaf, intricate wooden carvings, and rich and colorful paintings.

AN ADORNMENT AT THE TOP OF THE SHWEDAGON PAGODA IN MYANMAR CONTAINS AN ESTIMATED $3 BILLION WORTH OF GOLD AND JEWELS.

WHO BROUGHT ALL THAT BLING?

Legend says the glittering gold pagoda, an extravagant site to behold, is more than 2,600 years old. It was constructed after two brothers met the Buddha and were gifted with eight strands of his hair. The sacred hair was said to heal the deaf, cure the blind, and even cause gems to rain down from the sky. With the help of the king, the brothers began to build the Shwedagon Pagoda to honor the miracles.

If the legend is true, the Shwedagon Pagoda is the oldest Buddhist pagoda in the world. However, many scientists believe it was actually constructed between 1,100 and 1,500 years ago. Either way, the pagoda is an impressive engineering feat. It stands at 367 feet (112 m) tall, is adorned with nearly 60,000 pounds (27,220 kg) of gold and thousands of gems, and is protected by statues of lionlike leogryphs at each of its four entrances. With all this grandeur, it's definitely one of the most dazzling and decadent places in the world.

SREE PADMANABHASWAMY TEMPLE
Where: Thiruvananthapuram, India
Built: 500–300 B.C.
This temple is often called the richest in the world. It is said to have hidden inner chamber walls made of gold and undiscovered treasure.

GOLDEN PAVILION
Where: Kyoto, Japan
Built: Founded A.D. 1397, rebuilt A.D. 1955
Shining amid its peaceful natural surroundings, the Zen temple is a golden beacon of beauty. Each level displays a different style of architecture, and the pavilion is topped with a golden phoenix.

7 JAW-DROPPING FACTS ABOUT ...

LUCKY LANDMARKS

Need some **GOOD FORTUNE** for that upcoming exam? Consider taking a trip! **PEOPLE TRAVEL** far and wide to these amazing places around the world for a little extra luck.

Some people believe that **RUBBING THE PLAQUES** below the statue of **ST. JOHN OF BOHEMIA** on the Charles Bridge in Prague, Czechia (Czech Republic), **BRINGS GOOD LUCK.**

A set of shimmery **WINGED FIGURES** sit at the bottom of Hoover Dam, Nevada, U.S.A., where visitors **TOUCH THEIR BRONZE TOES** for good luck.

SPINNING THE TWO RINGS on the Schöner Brunnen fountain in Nuremberg, Germany, can supposedly bring good fortune.

THROWING A COIN with your right hand backward over your left shoulder into the **TREVI FOUNTAIN** in Rome, Italy, is said to grant good fortune.

If you **STICK YOUR THUMB** into the **"WEEPING COLUMN"** at the Hagia Sophia in Istanbul, Turkey, it might come out damp from the supposedly healing water that runs within it.

In Florence, Italy, **PLACING A COIN** in the mouth of a bronze statue of a boar and **RUBBING ITS SNOUT** is said to bring good fortune.

A stroll through paths lined with **DOZENS OF ORANGE** torii, or gates, at Fushimi Inari Taisha in Japan is said to **BRING SUCCESS** to your blossoming business.

Roman COLOSSEUM

FORGET A TIME MACHINE. If you want to visit ancient Rome, just head to the Colosseum! This sports arena opened its doors in the year A.D. 80. For the next four centuries, audiences of thousands gathered here to cheer on gladiator showdowns, parades, and other spectacles. The Colosseum has countless cool features. Here are a few of its stunning stats.

According to some records, the Colosseum was once flooded with water for a staged naval battle with **3,000** warriors.

Battered over time by earthquakes and storms, only **one-third** of the original Colosseum is standing.

It took **240,000** cartloads of stones just to build the arena's outside façade.

In 2017, an ancient Roman coin featuring the Colosseum sold for more than **$450,000.**

More than **4 million** tourists visit this site each year.

The floor had **36** trapdoors fighters could use to make surprise entrances.

To celebrate its opening, Emperor Titus held **100** days of gladiator matches.

It could seat around **50,000** spectators.

The Colosseum was built over part of an extravagant **300-room** underground palace created for Emperor Nero.

The original structure had some **80** entrances.

In 2013, archaeologists studying the Colosseum discovered **2,000-year-old** graffiti covering one passageway.

Which Wonder WOULD YOU CHOOSE?
PRAGUE CASTLE vs. HIMEJI CASTLE

Prague Castle and Himeji Castle are two of the most incredible castles in the entire world. Which would you rather visit?

PRAGUE CASTLE
Where: Czechia (Czech Republic)

Considered the largest ancient castle in the world, Prague Castle's first building was constructed in the ninth century. The castle has been added to, rebuilt, and redesigned due to multiple attacks, earthquakes, colossal fires, and also a number of new kings and leaders who took over and added their own special touches. Because of this, Prague Castle showcases different architectural styles and artistic features from many historical periods. The grounds hold multiple churches, defense towers, gardens, a vineyard, residences, and even museums—including a toy museum displaying toys from more than four centuries.

The presidents of Czechia (formerly Czechoslovakia) have held office here since 1918.

The castle grounds span 750,000 square feet (70,000 sq m).

The singing fountain in one of the gardens plays a rhythmic tune when water shoots from the jets and hits the bronze bowl below.

HIMEJI CASTLE
Where: Japan

This castle, the most visited and largest in Japan, is a force to be reckoned with! Unlike Prague Castle, the structure and grounds haven't changed much since it was built in its current style in the early 17th century. Incredibly durable, Himeji Castle has withstood multiple earthquakes, wars, attacks, and even a few major bombings over the years. It is also notorious for its amazingly advanced defense systems, with sneaky and ingenious elements laid throughout the grounds to puzzle and slow down invaders. For example, a lengthy, confusing maze that includes tall walls and multiple dead ends leads up to the main building. Good luck getting out!

Himeji Castle is also known as the White Heron Castle because the architecture resembles a heron taking flight.

The grounds include 83 buildings and are enclosed by three miles (4.8 km) of walls, as high as 85 feet (26 m) in some places.

One of the best times to visit is usually in the first few weeks of April, when the pink cherry blossom trees are in full bloom.

The hilltop the castle sits on was previously a sacred shrine.

Treasures of
KING TUT

King Tut's tomb contained a **TROVE OF RICHES**
to keep the pharaoh happy in the afterlife.
Discover **TUT'S COOLEST TREASURES.**

Tutankhamun ruled Egypt about 3,300 years ago.

BEDTIME

Tut's tomb held six beds, including a fold-up one for traveling! Another bed was gilded (covered in gold paint), and its legs were carved to resemble cat feet. The bed doesn't look too different from modern ones, but here's the kicker—the board at one end of the bed was where the feet went, not the head!

SNAZZY SANDALS

You may have a fancy pair of shoes for special occasions—but are they made of gold? Probably not! King Tut had solid-gold sandals that were placed on his feet before he was mummified. And this glitzy footwear isn't his only pair—archaeologists found around 80 shoes in the tomb!

MIGHTY MASK

King Tut's mask was created so his spirit would recognize his body after the two were separated in death. The 22.5-pound (10-kg) mask was made with two gold sheets that were hammered together, as well as colored glass and gemstones. The back of the mask was inscribed with a spell to guard Tut on his journey to the underworld, where the dead were thought to travel.

FANCY FALCON

Just because you're a mummy doesn't mean you can't wear bling! Tut's tomb included a necklace-like piece of jewelry made with gold and gemstones. Called a pectoral, it was worn over the chest. It was shaped as a falcon to represent the ancient Egyptian god Horus, known as the protector of pharaohs.

GAME ON!

Senet was a popular board game in ancient Egypt. Players tossed throwing sticks (a version of dice) to determine how many spaces to move their game pieces. The first player to move all their pawns to the finish won. Senet was buried with Tut to keep the pharaoh entertained.

STONE ➤
SNAPSHOTS

CHECK OUT PHOTOS OF
DIFFERENT SAN AGUSTÍN STATUES.

ONE REGION OF COLOMBIA HAS 600 STONE CARVINGS OF MYTHICAL CREATURES— AND NO ONE KNOWS EXACTLY WHO MADE THEM.

WHAT'S THE STORY BEHIND THESE STATUES?

San Agustín, Colombia, has some puzzling inhabitants: It's filled with hundreds of stone statues carved in the shape of gods and mythical creatures. They often sport huge fangs. Some are designed with headdresses and necklaces. And others clutch weapons such as clubs. Experts aren't exactly sure who sculpted the statues, some of which are up to 20 feet (6 m) tall. But they believe they were created for an important job—to guard the dead.

Some of the statues of San Agustín date back 2,000 years and were placed beside tombs. Scientists think the tombs contain the chieftains of an ancient culture that once lived in the area. The people of this society likely created the statues to protect their deceased leaders. Eventually, these people abandoned the area, leaving behind no written record of who they were. Perhaps the statues could tell us more about those who carved them—but they remain stone-faced, unwilling to spill any secrets!

⊙MODERN MARVELS

International Space Station

From sparkling cities and top-notch tree houses to cool pools and raucous roller coasters, the world's modern marvels are fantastic feats of creativity and design. But not only are these wonders a feast for the eyes—many of them have a very high fun factor, including an indoor tropical paradise and a museum devoted to dessert. Prepare yourself for the most exquisite, fun-filled jaw-droppers of the here and now.

SUPERCOOL
STRUCTURES

Can you say modern masterpieces? With their awe-inspiring designs, these structures really crank up the creativity. Check out some works of genius that have all the bells and whistles ... and then some!

Burj Khalifa

Where: United Arab Emirates

Burj Khalifa has some gasp-worthy stats. Rising 2,716.5 feet (828 m), it was the world's tallest building when it opened in 2010. At 551,000 tons (500,000 t), it's heavier than 70,000 African elephants. And if all its steel rods were laid end to end, they'd circle a quarter of Earth! The building also boasts one of the world's tallest observation decks on its 124th floor and superfast elevators that travel 22 miles an hour (36 km/h).

Nautilus House

Where: Mexico

One inventive architect designed his home to look like a shelled sea creature called the nautilus mollusk. The house has curved rooms and looping hallways, plus an indoor garden and a large front window with multicolored glass. If you lived here, you'd never want to come out of your shell.

Dragon Bridge

Where: Vietnam

This bridge is a little bonkers. The steel structure features a 1,864-foot (568-m) dragon that spans most of its length. Not only is the bridge decked out in 2,500 LED lights to make it glow in the dark, but it can also spew bursts of fire and jets of water from its "mouth." That's monstrously cool!

Treehotel

Where: Sweden

The small, sleek lodges of this Swedish hotel perch several feet above ground among the trees. One is cube-shaped with mirrored walls. One is shaped like a spaceship. It has portholes and a retractable staircase. Another resembles a bird's nest—designers built the exterior out of actual branches! Yet another suite is suspended from a small bridge and has an entrance at its top. Who wouldn't want to hang in these tree houses?

Lotus Temple

Where: India

This temple was designed to look like a lotus flower. It has 27 marble-and-concrete "petals" surrounding a central hall that can fit about 2,500 people. Like many real blooms, this human-made one relies on energy from the sun—solar panels provide the building with some of its power. Nine pools encircle the temple to make it seem as if it's floating on water, just as actual lotus flowers do.

Great Mosque of Djenné

Where: Mali

The Great Mosque of Djenné is the world's largest mud-built structure, big enough for 3,000 people! To create it, builders first baked mud-and-straw bricks. They then stacked the bricks to make the mosque's exterior. Finally, they covered everything in clay. Rain erodes parts of the mosque each year. So area residents hold an annual festival to make repairs.

Southern Cross Train Station

Where: Australia

It's easy to see why this building makes waves. The structure was designed with a wavy roof and ceiling. The shape has a purpose, aside from looking really cool. Hot air and train fumes travel upward, collecting in the highest parts of the ceiling. Then they are expelled through vents. That helps keep the station's air fresh.

Crooked House

Where: Poland

Turn on a fan—that building is melting! Well, not really. It only looks that way due to its wacky design. Known as Crooked House, the structure was based on drawings by a famous artist who illustrated Polish fairy tales.

Kansas City Public Library

Where: Missouri, U.S.A.

This looks like some heavy reading. The outside of the Kansas City Public Library was constructed to resemble a giant, packed bookshelf. There are 22 "books" shown in all, including *The Lord of the Rings* and *Charlotte's Web*. Each is about 25 feet (8 m) tall and nine feet (3 m) wide. Try fitting one of those in your backpack!

Tropical Islands

Where: Germany

Tropical Islands is a lavish water park built within a former airplane hangar in northern Germany. It features a sandy beach, an indoor rainforest that boasts 50,000 plants, and a huge pool with eight waterslides. You can even take hot-air balloon rides through the domed building, which rises higher than the Statue of Liberty.

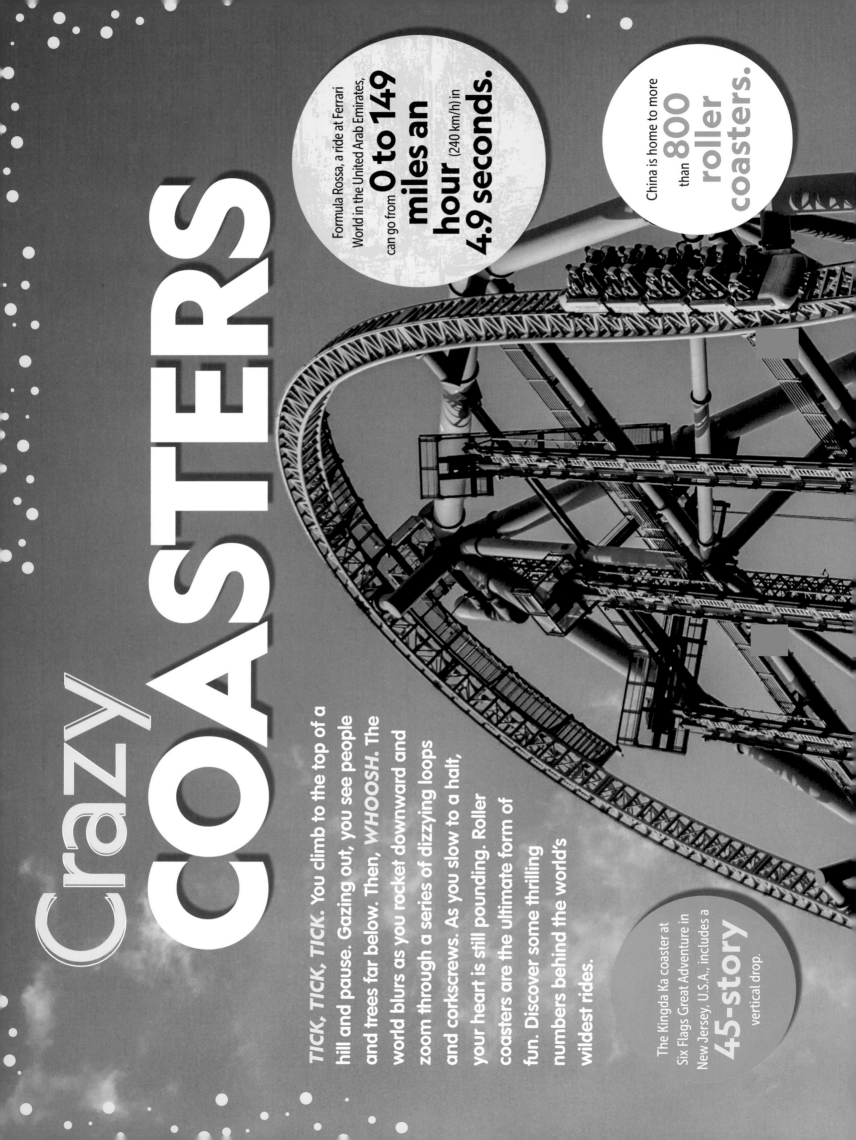

Crazy COASTERS

TICK, TICK, TICK. You climb to the top of a hill and pause. Gazing out, you see people and trees far below. Then, *WHOOSH.* The world blurs as you rocket downward and zoom through a series of dizzying loops and corkscrews. As you slow to a halt, your heart is still pounding. Roller coasters are the ultimate form of fun. Discover some thrilling numbers behind the world's wildest rides.

Formula Rossa, a ride at Ferrari World in the United Arab Emirates, can go from **0 to 149 miles an hour** (240 km/h) in **4.9 seconds.**

China is home to more than **800 roller coasters.**

The Kingda Ka coaster at Six Flags Great Adventure in New Jersey, U.S.A., includes a **45-story** vertical drop.

National Roller Coaster Day occurs in the United States each year on **August 16.**

With **8,133 feet** (2,479 m) **of track,** the Steel Dragon 2000 at Nagashima Spa Land in Japan could stretch the length of about 22 American football fields.

On the Time Traveler ride at Silver Dollar City in Missouri, U.S.A., cars **spin 360 degrees** as they zip down the track.

On one day in June 1994, **14 couples married** were on the Kumba roller coaster at Busch Gardens in Florida, U.S.A.

England's Smiler roller coaster at Alton Towers is decked out with **14 loops.**

Australia's Luna Park has operated the Great Scenic Railway roller coaster **since 1912.**

The Steel Curtain, a ride at Kennywood in Pennsylvania, U.S.A., flips you **upside down 9 times.**

At Gold Reef City in South Africa, passengers on the Tower of Terror elevator ride **drop 164 feet** (50 m), experiencing twice the gravitational force felt by astronauts during a rocket launch.

Kingda Ka roller coaster

87

Tokyo HOT➤ SPOTS

➤ **TOKYO IMPERIAL PALACE**
Japan's royals live here. NBD.

MORE PEOPLE LIVE IN TOKYO, JAPAN, THAN IN ALL OF AUSTRALIA.

HOW DID THIS MEGACITY GET SO PACKED?

Tokyo is one eye-popping place, filled with sparkling skyscrapers, colorful neon signs, and lots and lots of people. With more than 37 million residents, the greater Tokyo area is one of the most populated cities on Earth. This can make getting around, well, interesting. One Tokyo subway station gets more than 3.5 million commuters a day—that's about half the population of New York City! And trains throughout the system can become so packed that workers are hired to push passengers on board so the doors will close.

It wasn't always this way. Around the 12th century, Tokyo was a tiny fishing village called Edo. Over time, it grew into a large town with a glorious castle to boot. In 1868, a new emperor moved the national government to Edo, revamped the castle for his use, and renamed the city. Tokyo kept growing. Then, in the 20th century, the city was destroyed twice—first after an earthquake and again during World War II. Each time the city was rebuilt, its area expanded. This increase in size, along with an economic boom, eventually led to Tokyo becoming the colossal capital it is today.

CAT CAFÉS The city's many cat cafés serve beverages and snuggles.

TOKYO SKYTREE At 2,080 feet (634 m) high, it's one of the world's tallest towers.

SHIBUYA CROSSING This intersection is one of the world's busiest.

89

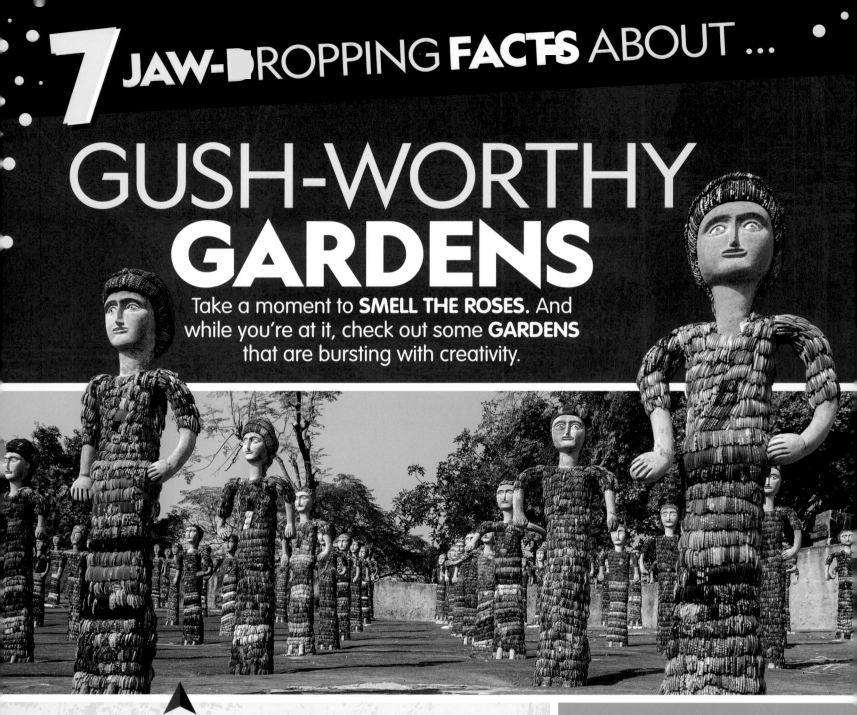

7 JAW-DROPPING **FACTS** ABOUT …

GUSH-WORTHY GARDENS

Take a moment to **SMELL THE ROSES.** And while you're at it, check out some **GARDENS** that are bursting with creativity.

The sculptures in India's **ROCK GARDEN OF CHANDIGARH** were made out of rocks and **RECYCLED TRASH.**

England's **ALNWICK POISON GARDEN** features **DEADLY PLANTS** that visitors aren't allowed to touch or smell.

THESE PLANTS CAN KILL

Every year, **800 VARIETIES** of **TULIPS** are planted in the **KEUKENHOF GARDENS** of Lisse, Netherlands.

ASTRONAUTS GROW VEGETABLES in a small chamber of the **INTERNATIONAL SPACE STATION.**

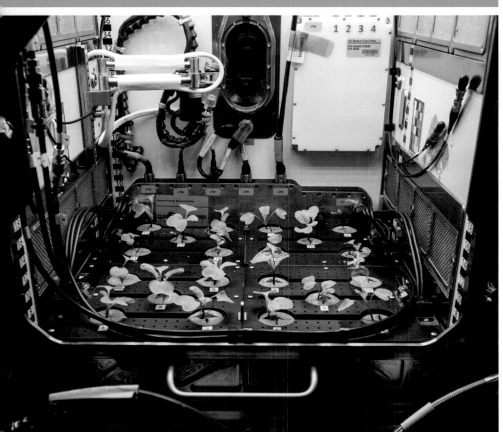

The **AUSTRALIAN BUTTERFLY SANCTUARY** in Kuranda Village, Australia, houses some **2,000 BUTTERFLIES** among its gardens.

DUBAI MIRACLE GARDEN in the United Arab Emirates has more than **60 MILLION FLOWERS** on display—the most of any garden on Earth.

The **PINEAPPLE GARDEN MAZE** in Hawaii, U.S.A., is a labyrinth of hedges with a pineapple-shaped garden at the center.

More EARTH
SNAPSHOTS >

LIGHTS AREN'T THE ONLY THINGS YOU CAN SEE ON OUR PLANET FROM SPACE. CHECK OUT OTHER EARTHLY OBJECTS AND EVENTS PHOTOGRAPHED BY SATELLITES ORBITING EARTH.

AT NIGHT, EARTH GLITTERS WITH **ARTIFICIAL LIGHT.**

HOW FAR AWAY CAN IT BE SEEN?

As dusk envelopes Earth, much of our planet begins to glow. The brightness is the result of artificial lighting from things like buildings and streetlamps. Using cutting-edge cameras on satellites, scientists can capture photos of these light shows. They can then combine images of various regions into one large picture to get a clear view of what entire continents and hemispheres look like at night. Unsurprisingly, packed cities produce the most glow and less populated rural areas the least. So scientists can use these images to better understand how people are spread out over the planet.

It's possible that Earth's lights could be seen from millions of miles away in space with a high-powered telescope. If a tech-savvy alien civilization is out there, maybe they can spot them! What's more, we might one day have strong enough telescopes to search for artificial light coming from alien cities on other planets. Isn't that illuminating?!

HURRICANE
Hurricanes are typically about 300 miles (483 km) wide.

VOLCANO
Volcanoes can blast materials 30,000 feet (9,144 m) into the air.

HIMALAYA
About 15,000 glaciers are located throughout the Himalaya range.

POOL PERF

The Marina Bay Sands building cost **$5.5 BILLION** to construct. It includes a hotel with more than **2,500 ROOMS, 270 SHOPS, A MUSEUM,** multiple **THEATERS,** and much more.

el Concierge

EXIT

To make the pool, builders used **422,000 POUNDS (191,400 kg)** of stainless **STEEL.** All together, the steel weighs as much as 30 full-grown African elephants.

More COOL POOLS

◄ BADESCHIFF
Berlin, Germany
This floating pool, which is covered in cold weather, sits in the Spree River.

◄ HANGING GARDENS POOL
Bali, Indonesia
Built on two levels, this resort pool overlooks a lush jungle.

ECTION

Talk about a high dive! When you splash into the water here, you're entering one of the highest swimming pools on Earth. It perches atop the Marina Bay Sands building in Singapore. Find out why this pool rules.

The swimming pool is ON TOP of the 57-STORY BUILDING.

Not only is this pool high up, it's also the LONGEST elevated pool in the world, stretching 492 FEET (150 m). That's about the length of FIVE BASKETBALL COURTS!

Eek! This swimming pool looks like it has NO FRONT RIM. The rim is there, but water flowing over the edge hides it from view. This water splashes into a basin and is pumped back into the pool.

It holds 380,000 GALLONS (1,438,456 L) of water.

◄ **SANTORINI CAVE POOL**
Santorini, Greece
Sitting on a cliff edge above the Aegean Sea, this hotel pool is tucked in a cave.

◄ **SAN ALFONSO DEL MAR POOL**
Algarrobo, Chile
This enormous pool is bigger than 15 American football fields.

≪ HOI AN, VIETNAM

Hoi An may have been coated in yellow because the color symbolizes luck in Vietnamese culture. Yellow also absorbs less sunlight than other shades. The coating could help keep buildings in this tropical region cool.

FAROE ISLANDS ≫

This might make you green with envy. Many houses on the Faroe Islands, which lie south of Iceland, sport cool-looking grass-covered roofs! The roofs provide insulation, keeping the homes toasty in chilly weather.

COLORFUL

MENTON, FRANCE ≫

Shades of orange cover buildings in Menton year-round. And once a year, the city gets *even more* orange! It holds an annual citrus festival with fruit sculptures made from 140 tons (127 t) of oranges, tangerines, and lemons.

SANTORINI, GREECE

Like the yellow buildings in Hoi An, the white ones of Santorini reflect sunlight to prevent overheating. Whitewash, the paint mixture coating the houses, is also a disinfectant that might have been used to help stop the spread of disease during plagues.

FALUN, SWEDEN

Falun is home to copper mines where red pigment has been extracted to make house paint for at least 500 years. Today, the color is popular in Falun and across Sweden. But at first, the paint was so pricey only royals and nobility could afford it.

LIVING

Here in these towns, it's all about the hues.

CHEFCHAOUEN, MOROCCO

Some believe this city was painted blue because the color has a reputation for repelling mosquitoes. It's also possible the blue is meant to represent the sky and heavens.

JAIPUR, INDIA

In 1876, a British prince paid a visit to Jaipur. To honor him, the city was painted pink, a color that traditionally represents hospitality in Indian culture. After the prince left, the color stuck around.

MAGNIFICENT MUSEUMS

Chihuly Garden and Glass museum

Think museums just hold **treasures** of the past? Think again! Some museums are dedicated to today's **coolest artistic creations.** Others offer **wacky experiences.** And still others pay tribute to some of our favorite things—like **dessert!** Check out a few museums with attractions that make them must-see **modern marvels.**

Blown glass art at Chihuly Garden and Glass museum

GLASS GALORE

This glass-filled spot shatters all expectations! The Chihuly Garden and Glass museum in Seattle, Washington, U.S.A., is home to dozens of incredible glass artworks. Inside one room, you'll find a 100-foot (30-m)-long sculpture made of 1,340 glass plates suspended from the ceiling. In another room, glass starfish, sea urchins, and octopuses perch on an enormous blue-and-green tower. Outside the building sits a 16-foot (4.8-m)-wide glass sculpture of the sun. The grounds also feature a "garden" filled with glass roses.

How did artist Dale Chihuly and his team make these masterpieces? To create such sculptures, glass is heated on a metal rod until it's a molten blob. Then the artists, called glassblowers, blow air through the rod and into the material to shape it. The end result is some first-class glass.

UNDERSEA MUSEUM

Forget a ticket—to get close to the art in this museum, you need scuba gear. Located off the coast of Cancún, Mexico, the Cancún Underwater Museum lies 30 feet (9 m) underwater. It's made up of around 500 sculptures of people and objects.

The six artists who created the sculptures didn't just want to wow visitors. Their main goal was to help rebuild a damaged reef in the area. So, they made their sculptures with a type of cement that allows algae and coral to grow on the surface. One of the sculptures was even built with openings

for lobsters to enter and shelves on which they can sleep—sort of like a lobster hotel! The artists hope the undersea museum inspires visitors to care for the ocean.

SWEET SPOT

The Dessert Museum in Manila, the Philippines, is a real treat. To enter, you pass through a doughnut-shaped opening and glide down a pink slide. The inside boasts several rooms devoted to a variety of goodies, including cotton candy, gummy bears, marshmallows, doughnuts, ice cream, and cake pops.

No one would blame you if your mouth started watering during your trip. Good thing there are plenty of samples to try. And in the cotton candy room, you can even pluck handfuls of the sticky stuff right from the exhibit! The museum doesn't just offer sugar, though. Visitors can play games such as hopscotch and learn fun facts about dessert. Now that's a recipe for a good time!

OTHER UNUSUAL MUSEUMS INCLUDE THE AVANOS HAIR MUSEUM OF TURKEY, THE BRITISH LAWNMOWER MUSEUM OF ENGLAND, AND THE SALT AND PEPPER SHAKER MUSEUM OF TENNESSEE, U.S.A.

THE WORLD'S OLDEST KNOWN MUSEUM WAS BUILT 2,500 YEARS AGO IN WHAT IS NOW IRAQ.

Cancún Underwater Museum

Wacky
RESEARCH ▶
STATIONS
DISCOVER COOL SCIENCE CENTERS!

◀ **BIOSPHERE 2**
Based in Arizona, U.S.A., this facility houses a model rainforest and a coastal fog desert, among other biomes.

AT ONE FACILITY IN UTAH, U.S.A., PEOPLE PRETEND TO LIVE ON MARS.

WHY WAS THIS MARS-LIKE HABITAT CREATED?

A person in a space suit descends from a white pod and bounces across the dusty ground. Hopping on an all-terrain vehicle, she sets off to explore the rust-colored landscape. This isn't an astronaut on the red planet. It's a scientist at the Mars Desert Research Station (MDRS) in southeast Utah.

A group called the Mars Society set up MDRS in 2001. They placed it in a region of Utah with a terrain similar to that of the red planet. The research station hosts crews who simulate a Mars mission and includes a pod with living quarters, labs, observatories, and a greenhouse. The goal is to prepare for future trips to Mars. Researchers at MDRS test equipment and carry out experiments. And while there, they must wear their space suits whenever they go outside, just as they would on Mars. A little slice of Martian life right here on Earth? That's out of this world!

JANG BOGO STATION
This South Korean–operated station in Antarctica is built to withstand winds of 145 miles an hour (234 km/h).

INTERNATIONAL SPACE STATION
In this station, which orbits 250 miles (400 km) above Earth, astronauts have studied how to grow plants in space, among other experiments.

Which Wonder WOULD YOU CHOOSE?
HOT-AIR BALLOON EATERY vs. ICE-FILLED RESTAURANT

Check out two delectable dining establishments and decide where you'd most like to grab a bite.

HOT-AIR BALLOON EATERY
Where: Netherlands

CuliAir Skydining takes dining to new heights. This sky-high restaurant inside a hot-air balloon can fit 10 people and has counters and a food-preparation station. As the balloon soars over the Dutch countryside, the chef whips up a three-course meal. The coolest part? The chef uses heat from the hot-air balloon to cook. Uncooked food is placed in containers and, using a pulley system, is raised to the top of the balloon. Here, the burning flame that helps the balloon fly also simmers the dinner. Once cooked, the food is lowered from the top of the balloon to the basket, where it is served to the passengers.

The CuliAir travels up to 6,500 feet (2,000 m) above the ground.

This balloon trip lasts about an hour and a half.

ICE-FILLED RESTAURANT
Where: United Arab Emirates

This restaurant, located in the city of Dubai, may give you chills—literally! The inside of the Chillout Lounge is made of ice, including ice seats, tables, and sculptures. Visitors will even find ice curtains and picture frames! The temperature in the Chillout Lounge is set at 21°F (-6°C) to prevent the frozen interior from melting. That's quite a difference from the temperatures outside, which regularly surpass 100°F (38°C) in summer. It also means diners will want to bulk up with the winter coats, hats, and scarves that the restaurant offers. To make guests extra cozy, they're given drinks like tea and hot chocolate upon entering the restaurant. No wonder this place has become a hot spot!

The Chillout Lounge isn't the only wintry place in Dubai—visitors can also go to an indoor ski resort located in a shopping mall.

The restaurant welcomes about 100 visitors a day.

Ice sculptures in the restaurant are carved in the shape of camels, hearts, penguins, and more!

CHAPTER 5

SPECTACU SPACE

Orion Nebula

LAR

Strange planets, dancing space dust, sparkly meteor showers—the universe surprises and amazes us with fantastic phenomena. Amid the light show lies a vast darkness riddled with unanswered questions that continues to lure us beyond Earth. With scientists building rockets that could take us to Mars and researching the tiniest signs of life, it's clear there's a lot left to explore.

RINGS MORE

An **EXOPLANET** is a planet **OUTSIDE** of our **SOLAR SYSTEM**.

J1407b's rings, which were discovered in 2012, stretch **75 MILLION MILES** (120 million km).

Like Saturn's rings, J1407b's rings have **GAPS**, which means **MOONS** have likely formed around the planet.

ASTRONOMERS THEORIZED that the rings around **JUPITER** and **SATURN** appeared at an early stage of the planets' development, but this theory wasn't proved until the **DISCOVERY OF J1407B**.

More **EXOTIC** EXOPLANETS

◄ GJ 504b
Exoplanet GJ 504b is so vibrantly magenta that it looks like it came from a galactic gumball machine. This gas giant balloons an estimated four times larger than Jupiter—our solar system's biggest planet.

◄ PSR J1719-1438 b
The name PSR J1719-1438 b might not dazzle, but this planet is a diamond about five times larger than Earth.

SUPER
THAN SATURN'S

Bring on the rings! An exoplanet called J1407b hundreds of light-years from Earth has a ring system that stretches 200 times farther than Saturn's. What does this number mean for us Earthlings? Saturn's rings are the largest in our solar system, but we need a telescope to see them. If planet J1407b spun in Saturn's celestial spot, its massive halo of rings would make it appear to be several times the size of a full moon in the nighttime sky!

J1407b is only **16 MILLION YEARS OLD, while** Saturn is **4.6 BILLION YEARS OLD.**

As more **MOONS AND SATELLITES** form from the ring particles, astronomers expect the rings to disappear in **SEVERAL MILLION YEARS.**

HD 189733b
On planet HD 189733b, it rains sharp blades of molten glass, and wind speeds are seven times faster than the speed of sound.

PSR B1620-26 b
Almost three times as old as Earth, planet PSR B1620-26 b is the oldest known planet in the universe.

PLASMA BALLS FROM THE SUN ≫

Cannonball! Stay clear of any explosive splashes, though. Plasma, fiery balls of charged particles, use an enormous amount of heat and energy to race around the sun at 125,000 miles an hour (201,170 km/h) until they explode.

≪ NEPTUNE

Hold on to your hats, because this icy blue giant is the windiest planet in our solar system, with wind speeds faster than the speed of sound. Conversely, the rate at which it orbits the sun is quite slow—one year on this snail of a planet is equal to 165 Earth years.

The MAJESTIC

WHEN GALAXIES ≫ COLLIDE

When one galaxy collides with another, the larger swallows the smaller, creating a bigger galaxy. In fact, the monstrous Milky Way wasn't its familiar large spiral shape until it digested a galaxy a fourth of its size some 10 billion years ago.

RCW 120

This glowing green bubble—created by the most massive type of star in the universe—can only be seen with NASA's Spitzer Space Telescope. Infrared wavelengths assign different colors to this formation.

≪ RED DWARFS

The smallest type of star, numerous red dwarfs speckle our sky, though their light is too dim for the human eye to see from Earth. But their star power still shines—red dwarfs make up the majority of our galaxy, and they outlive any other type of star!

MILKY WAY

Our own galaxy is made of billions of perplexing pieces—planets with wild weather, nebulae (clouds of gas and space dust) full of color, and new stars being born, to name just a few.

SATURN HEXAGON ≫

These peachy pastel clouds hovering above Saturn's north pole surprised scientists with their perfect hexagonal shape. When spotted, the storm looked blue. This color-changing curiosity could be due to the different seasons in which it was viewed from Cassini, a probe sent into space.

≪ ORION NEBULA

Baby stars are being born in this cloud, one of the star clusters most visible from Earth. Four main stars known as the Trapezium are the brightest, but the colorful curtain of dust could be hiding up to 1,000 more sparkling lights.

SUPERHERO SPACE SUIT

Space is harsh on the human body, so it makes sense that astronauts would need a suit with superhero standards to keep them safe while on a space walk—when they leave a spacecraft to explore. The suit has multiple layers and cool controls, and not just for regulating astronauts' body temperature. It's strong enough to withstand blows from particles hurtling through space and provides astronauts with oxygen and water.

The helmet's TRANSLUCENT VISOR is made with a thin LAYER OF REAL GOLD that protects astronauts from the sun but still allows them to see.

FINGERS are the part of the body that get the coldest the fastest, so the glove tips have LITTLE HEATERS to keep fingers warm.

CAMERAS can be attached to the helmet so that NASA scientists on Earth can see what the astronaut sees.

SPACE WALKS are usually FIVE TO EIGHT HOURS long.

Astronauts go on space walks to conduct EXPERIMENTS AND FIX EQUIPMENT, from repairing satellites to REPLACING BATTERIES on the International Space Station.

CORDS attach to the waist bearer, tethering astronauts to the spacecraft so they don't drift into space.

The space suit is difficult to move in, so the LOWER TORSO has a ring around it called a WAIST BEARER that allows the astronaut to twist their body as needed.

The most important piece of the suit, the PORTABLE LIFE SUPPORT SYSTEM, or PLSS, provides astronauts with OXYGEN, WATER, A BATTERY, A TWO-WAY RADIO, and A WARNING SYSTEM if the suit malfunctions.

When on a space walk, astronauts can go to the BATHROOM IN THEIR SPACE SUIT.

If an astronaut becomes disconnected from a tether, the SAFER is a tool located on the back of the suit. It has SMALL JETS used to fly back to the spacecraft.

7 **JAW**-DROPPING **FACTS** ABOUT ...

SPACE
SHOWSTOPPERS

These **EXTRAORDINARY EVENTS** and **STELLAR OBJECTS** can often be seen from Earth without a telescope.

The **INTERNATIONAL SPACE STATION** can be seen zooming through the sky, orbiting Earth every 90 minutes.

A **COMET** is a giant **SPACE SNOWBALL** made of frozen gas, rock, and dust left over from when our solar system was created 4.6 billion years ago.

A **SUPERMOON** is a full moon that occurs when **THE MOON'S ORBIT IS CLOSEST TO EARTH,** making it look bigger and brighter than the average full moon.

A **SOLAR ECLIPSE** is when the moon blocks out the sun—the sun looks like a **RING OF FIRE** in the sky.

The **PERSEID METEOR SHOWER,** which occurs from mid-July through August, has the most numerous and brightest meteors— or **SHOOTING STARS.**

SATURN'S reoccurring thunderstorms, called the **GREAT WHITE SPOTS,** last several months and are large enough to see with a telescope.

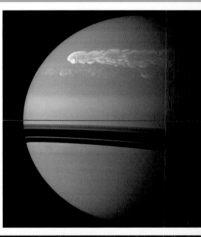

When planets in our **SOLAR SYSTEM** are opposite the sun, they **SHINE BRIGHTER** in the night sky.

Surprising
SNAPSHOTS

Check out the UNBELIEVABLE PHENOMENA caught ON CAMERA.

BLACK HOLE

Black holes gobble up anything that gets too close, from entire stars to the fastest-moving element in space—light! Though there are likely more than one billion black holes in the Milky Way, scientists didn't capture an image of one until 2019. It took eight telescopes scattered around the globe working simultaneously to snap this groundbreaking shot in 2019. The black hole in the photo is 6.5 billion times the mass of our sun.

Black holes are so dense that light cannot escape—the bright ring in the picture is gas and particles orbiting the black hole, making the black hole visible.

"PILLARS OF CREATION"

In this famous photograph taken by the Hubble Space Telescope, new stars are exploding into existence within monstrous towers of swirling space dust. Though it may look like just another cloud in the sky, the tallest of the three pillars is a whopping four light-years tall—that's trillions of miles! To put this space-speak into perspective, the closest star to Earth is our sun, which is only 93 million miles (150 million km) from us—just a teeny-tiny fraction of one single light-year.

FERMI BUBBLES

In 2010, scientists discovered that the Milky Way is sandwiched between two giant bubbles. These aren't like bath bubbles—together they extend outward at tens of thousands of light-years! Though scientists are still stumped by their origin and purpose, they do know that these bubbles are filled with fast-flying gamma rays that rush out of the center of the Milky Way at two million miles an hour (3.2 million km/h).

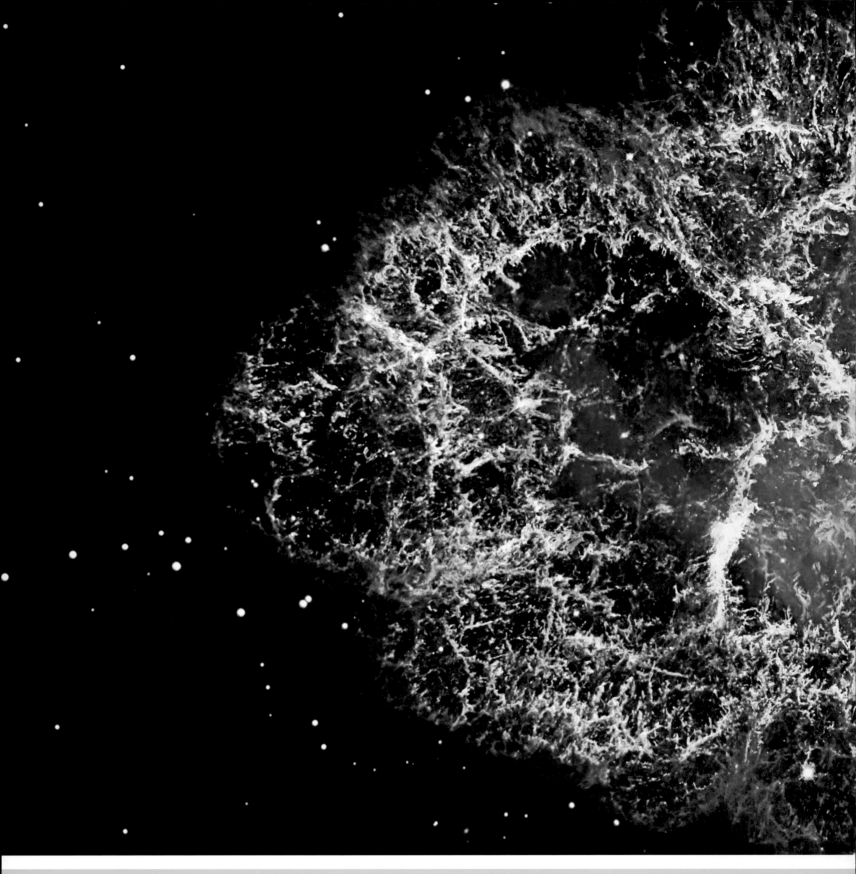

A RAINBOW of DWARF STARS

RED
As the longest living stars, they are often used to calculate the age of star clusters.

A STAR EXPLODES SOMEWHERE IN THE UNIVERSE ABOUT EVERY SECOND.

WHERE DOES ALL THAT STARDUST GO?

All stars will die, but only the mightiest ones end in an explosive fire-works show called a supernova. Compared to a smaller star, a massive star has a number of elements in and around its core that fuel the star and keep its big gravitational pull in balance. When it starts to lose these elements, gravity pulls the heaviest elements inward, making the core denser and blazing hot.

At first, it may look like the star is growing instead of dying, as the outside layers become much lighter, and the core's intense heat makes them balloon outward. But the core becomes so hot and dense with iron that it explodes, blasting an array of heavy elements, particles, and dust into the universe at 9,000 to 25,000 miles a second (15,000 to 40,000 km/s).

This matter hurtling through space makes up the building blocks for the universe. Not only do they help create new star formations, but they also provide our planet—and us—with iron. That's right—we're walking and talking parts of the universe's coolest fireworks show!

WHITE
These small but nearly dead stars are some of the densest objects in the universe.

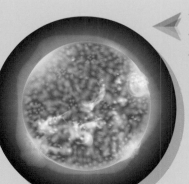

YELLOW
These are fiery medium-size stars, like our sun.

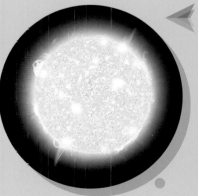

BLUE
In theory, when red dwarf stars are at the end of their life, they will get extremely hot for a burst of time, shining blue.

7 JAW-DROPPING **FACTS** ABOUT ...
THE HUBBLE SPACE TELESCOPE

HUBBLE isn't your average telescope. For one thing, it **FLOATS ABOVE EARTH!** Launched into space in 1990, it **TAKES PHOTOS** of the universe and transmits them to a **CONTROL CENTER** on the ground. Check out **STELLAR FACTS** about this device.

The telescope is **43.5 FEET** (13.3 m) long—that's about as **LONG AS A BUS.** ▶

This **SOLAR-POWERED** telescope uses an average of **2,100 WATTS OF ELECTRICITY,** about the same as five refrigerators. ▼

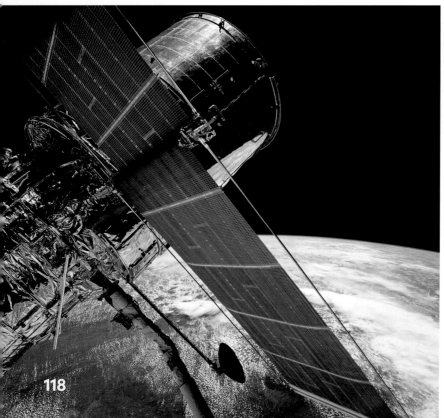

Carina Nebula

Hubble can **"SEE"** objects more than **13 BILLION LIGHT-YEARS AWAY.**

Hubble weighs about **27,000 POUNDS** (12,247 kg)—nearly the same as **TWO ADULT AFRICAN ELEPHANTS.**

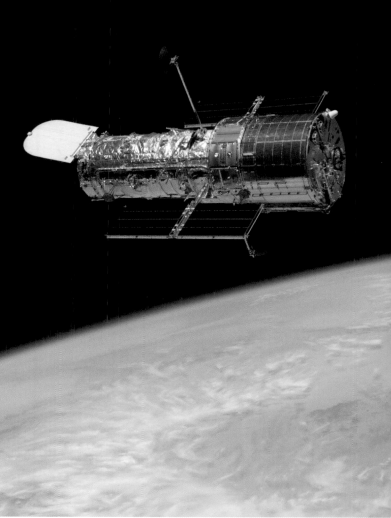

The device has made more than **1.3 MILLION OBSERVATIONS** since it was **LAUNCHED IN 1990.**

It **ORBITS** at a speed of **17,000 MILES AN HOUR** (27,300 km/h), circling Earth every 97 minutes.

Hubble discovered four of **PLUTO'S FIVE MOONS.**

Charon, one of Pluto's moons

Marvelous
MARS

NAMED AFTER THE ROMAN GOD OF WAR, Mars (also known as the red planet) does indeed look bloodstained from battle. In fact, its soil is rich with a mineral that is found in blood: iron. But did you know our ruby-colored neighbor has blue sunsets? Or that it's the only other planet besides Earth with polar ice caps? In fact, humans could call Mars home someday because of these ice caps, as there is evidence of a lake under one of them. Tall glass of fresh drinking water, anyone?

Mars only has **37 percent** of the gravity that Earth has—you could jump nearly **3 times** higher on Mars.

A canyon called Valles Marineris is **2,500 miles** (4,000 km) long. On Earth, it would span all of North America and then some—the Grand Canyon is only **277 miles** (446 km) long.

Mars is the **4th** planet from the sun.

It has **2** moons—Phobos and Deimos—that were discovered in **1877.**

Scientists found evidence of a lake about **1 mile** (1.6 km) below the planet's south polar ice cap that could be **12 miles** (19 km) wide.

Because Mars takes longer to orbit the sun than Earth does, a year on Mars lasts **687** Earth days.

Olympus Mons is the tallest mountain in our solar system at an estimated **14 miles** (22 km) high—and it's a volcano that may still be active!

In roughly **70 million** years, Phobos could break apart and become a set of rings.

Large dust storms that cover the whole planet will happen every **5.5 Earth years,** with winds as fast as **60 miles an hour** (97 km/h).

MOON ➤
MAGIC
CHECK OUT FUN FACTS ABOUT THIS SATELLITE.

The moon is about one-fourth the size of Earth.

WHEN APOLLO 11 ASTRONAUTS WERE LANDING THEIR LUNAR MODULE ON THE MOON, THEY HAD ONLY 30 SECONDS OF FUEL LEFT.

HOW WERE THEY ABLE TO MAKE THE DESCENT?

For three days, Apollo 11 barreled through space. It was mid-July 1969, and the spacecraft was headed to the moon. Two of the astronauts on board would be the first people to walk on its surface. After entering the moon's orbit, the crew prepared to touch down. Astronaut Michael Collins would remain in orbit in the spacecraft's command module. Meanwhile, Neil Armstrong and Buzz Aldrin would descend to the moon's surface in a lunar module called the *Eagle*.

After detaching from the rest of the craft, Armstrong steered the module downward. But toward the end of the two-hour descent, he realized they had a problem: They were burning more fuel than planned. A warning light switched on, and alarms dinged. The astronauts knew that if they didn't land soon, they would have to abort the mission. So the pair hunkered down and concentrated on the landing. Finally, they came to rest on the moon's surface—with 30 seconds of fuel to spare. After about 21 hours on the moon, it was time to leave. Launching a rocket motor, the astronauts took off and rejoined the main spacecraft. Then the heroes of Apollo 11 journeyed home.

Apollo 11 traveled at 2,040 miles an hour (3,280 km/h).

It takes 27.3 days for the moon to orbit Earth.

Temperatures on the moon can rise as high as 260°F (127°C) and dip as low as minus 280°F (-173°C).

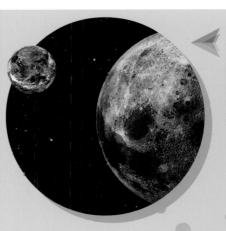

The moon is drifting 1.5 inches (3.8 cm) away from Earth each year.

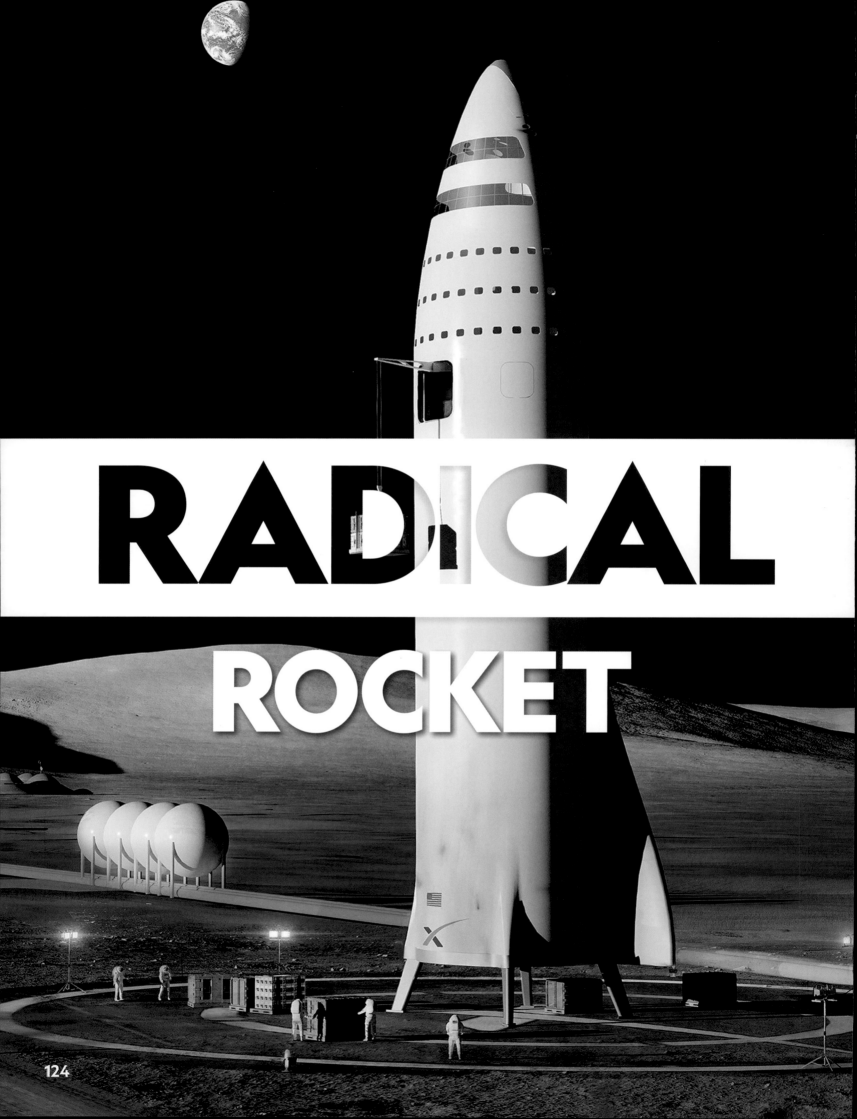

RADICAL
ROCKET

Get ready to **blast off** with the most powerful rocket ever built—the **SpaceX Starship.** This stellar spacecraft is making space travel possible for tourists, **igniting imaginations** around the globe. Founder (and space optimist) Elon Musk started SpaceX with the ultimate goal of getting humans to **Mars.** However, Starship also plans to go to the **moon** and other **space destinations.**

STARSHIP WAS ORIGINALLY CALLED MARS COLONIAL TRANSPORTER (MCT).

FANTASTIC FEATURES

The Starship is decked out with features unlike any other spacecraft. Standing 160 feet (50 m) tall, it's ready to carry 100 passengers. Almost all rockets of the past have been single-use, but this reusable spacecraft has the capability to fly into space at least 12 times.

SPACE TOURISM

Ready to take a flight on this stellar spacecraft yet? What if we told you that with SpaceX technology it will take only 80 days to get to Mars? That's quite a feat, considering that it would take an estimated six to nine months using NASA's current technology. Plus, with a restaurant and a movie theater on board, the Starship is sure to keep guests busy while they ride.

LIVING ON ANOTHER PLANET

SpaceX isn't just looking to send people on a vacation to Mars. It plans to have people live there. Many of the first ships will carry the tools and people that can build and establish a city there. If creating the space city of their dreams goes as planned, it will cost an estimated $100,000 to $500,000 for the average human to move to Mars. Such a move cannot be taken lightly! Though it may take a mere 80 days to get there, ships will only be launched to and from Mars every 26 months, when Earth and Mars are at their closest and most ideal distance for travel. So if you move there, prepare to stay for at least two years!

THE LAST TIME HUMANS LANDED ON THE MOON WAS DURING NASA'S APOLLO 17 TRIP IN 1972.

WATERY
WONDERS

Thor's Well, Oregon, U.S.A.

Beneath wild ocean waves and crystal clear lakes lies a wondrous world full of sea creatures with superpowers, lost ancient cities, and underwater forests. Water makes our world dazzling and diverse, from rivers that run red to supersalty seas that make us feel like we're floating on air. Best of all, there's still so much to discover!

WACKY WATERS

Journey around the world to discover a treasure of wild, watery gems: colors you never dreamed water could be, unbelievable structures that water creates, and adaptable animals that figure out the most creative ways to survive in it.

Red Sea Glowing Coral

Where: Middle East

Feast your eyes on color-changing power at its finest! Coral is an animal, and like any living creature, it needs food to survive. Do you know what a coral's favorite snack is? Light! Red Sea glowing coral live deep in the water, which makes it more difficult for light to reach them. But when it does, the coral captures it. There's one problem—the imprisoned light is blue, and therefore weak food for these corals. So, as the coral absorbs the blue light, a special protein in the coral's tissue turns the blue light into stronger red light. Thanks to this color-changing protein, these deep-sea creatures will live much longer lives.

Thor's Well

Where: Oregon, U.S.A.

Rumor has it that a sinkhole in Oregon, U.S.A., will transport you to the underworld. Carved into the coastline's craggy black rock left over from fiery volcanic eruptions thousands of years ago, a sinkhole called Thor's Well can be seen at high tide. During high tide, ocean waves crash into the well and get sucked into the depths below. But what may look like a bottomless hole is actually only 20 feet (6 m) deep, and the ocean floor feeds the water back into the wild waves.

Bahamas Blue Holes

Where: Bahamas

Get ready to explore an underwater cave full of secrets! Blue holes are one of the most unique habitats in the world. In the Bahamas alone, there are more than 1,000 blue holes, but scientists and divers alike have to be extremely careful while diving in them. The holes can be super deep and narrow, making it hard for light to reach the bottom. With little light, there is little oxygen, which makes it a difficult home for life but a perfect environment for preserving the past. Scientists often find astounding ancient fossils at the bottom, along with sediment that provides insight into weather patterns dating back hundreds of years.

The Heart of Voh, Le Coeur de Voh

Where: New Caledonia

Visitors fall in love with this magnificent heart-shaped mangrove swamp. In a mangrove, shrubs look like they are floating on top of the water, but they actually have roots that twist and wind their way to the muddy bottom. The heart shape is held together by the roots, and is best viewed from high above. Also impressive? This mangrove swamp lies at the edge of one of the world's largest and most diverse marine parks. Sharks, whales, turtles, and one of the largest coral reefs thrive there—a heartening sight to behold.

The Red River, El Río Tinto

Where: Spain

Whoa—is that river made of blood? What may look like something straight out of a horror movie is actually the result of hundreds of years of mining. The surrounding land was once filled with a fortune—copper, gold, and silver. The large amounts of acid and heavy metals in the river have rendered the area extremely toxic. It might as well be covered in bright yellow caution tape!

Mud Volcanoes

Where: Gobustan, Azerbaijan

More than 300 monstrous mud volcanoes bubble and explode with toxic gas across this otherworldly landscape. Unlike volcanoes that spew hot lava, mud volcanoes brew bubbles cold to the touch. But if a lot of gas escapes from the mud, it can cause the volcano to blast fiery flames for days, filling the air with deadly gas and blobs of mud and dust. Azerbaijan has the highest concentration of active mud volcanoes in the world, including two of the largest—Boyuk Khanizadagh and Turaghai—and many that exist underwater in the Caspian Sea.

Frozen Bubbles of Lake Abraham

Where: Alberta, Canada

These bubbles could cause a fire! Trapped within a frozen lake, they are filled with a gas called methane. How did the methane get there? The top part of Lake Abraham freezes in the winter, but the bottom part does not. It's full of fish, thriving plants, and the creatures that create those frozen bubbles—bacteria! When animals and plants die, they fall to the bottom of the lake, which makes a hearty meal for the bacteria. Once the bacteria have had their fill, they release a gas that bubbles toward the surface and freezes on its way up. That's one bubble you don't want to pop!

Baatara Gorge Waterfall

Where: Lebanon

Welcome to the disappearing waterfall show! One month you'll see an 837-foot (255-m) stream of water fall from a cliff, pass through three natural bridges, and plunge into a cave below. The next month—poof—it's gone. That's because for most of the year, the surrounding area on top of the plateau is covered in snow and is too cold for any water to run. Come March and April, when spring warms the air, the snow finally melts, cascading off the ancient limestone cliff and dazzling visitors with its daring drop.

Mono Lake

Where: California, U.S.A.

In an extremely salty one-million-year-old lake, spires eerily jut out from the water like tips of an ancient sunken castle. But these towers are actually made of minerals, built up over time from springs on the lake floor that pump freshwater into the lake. While you enjoy the scenery, dare to take a dip: The high salt concentration makes humans and animals easily float! During your visit, you might paddle past a special species of brine shrimp—trillions of them thrive in Mono Lake. The result is a bird-watching paradise, as millions of birds flock to the lake to dine on the tiny morsels of salty meat.

Crater Lakes at Kelimutu Volcano

Where: Indonesia

Has a lake ever changed colors right before your eyes? It might sound like magic, but three lakes that sit at the crest of Kelimutu volcano do just that. In fact, each lake can be a different color at one time: creamy white, dark blood red, or vibrant blue. NASA fondly refers to the lakes as "volcanic mood rings" because the color of each lake is based on the amount of oxygen in the steam that blows off the surface.

Travertine Pools

Where: Huanglong, China

From above, it might look like a dragon is snaking its way through the forested Huanglong Valley in Huanglong National Park. In reality, the ribbon of yellow spanning 2.2 miles (3.5 km) is a series of natural turquoise-colored pools carved into a yellow rock called travertine. The cascading pools formed over thousands of years, and now people come from far and wide to relax in the mineral-filled water in one of the most picturesque places in the world. Often called "Fairy Land on Earth," it's surrounded by glacier-topped mountains, towering bamboo, and one of China's most beloved creatures—the giant panda.

SNOWMELT
MAGIC

Under frozen **landscapes** of sparkling white lies an **explosion of color** and life waiting to **burst forth.**

SUMMER SURPRISE

Snowmelt is like a birthday present that spring is eager to unwrap. As the sun warms the ground and the snow starts to melt, the surprise is finally revealed. Water meanders down hillsides, transforming rivers from trickling streams to raging rapids, changing dry land into liquid-packed lakes, and filling reservoirs with drinking water. Best of all, it changes nature into a miraculous show of color, wonder, and an abundance of life big and small.

Mount Rainier, the star of Mount Rainier National Park in Washington, U.S.A., is covered in 25 major glaciers year-round, but every summer the surrounding snowfields melt, revealing a stunning show of wildflowers. A rainbow of color, dozens of different species spread like wildfire across the land. But you have to be quick to catch them: Just when the snow finally melts in July, the first flower-killing frost descends in August.

UNDERWATER PARK

On the other side of the world in Austria, a serene park has a secret. It sits in a valley surrounded by snowy mountains with plenty of park benches, walking paths, tall trees, and a small pond. But in summer, the snow on the mountaintops melts, transforming the park below into a lake. Called Green Lake, it's deep enough for scuba divers to swim the walking paths of the park, skim over wooden bridges, and sit against a tree underwater, as if in a dream.

GLACIER SURFING

Our trip around the world ends in the land of ice—the Arctic. The Arctic is home to a wide variety of animals that count on glaciers to survive. Glaciers are made of compacted snow that builds up over years, and they continue to grow larger in the winter. When it becomes slightly warmer in the Arctic, pieces of glaciers break off. Animals surf around the Arctic on the broken glacier chunks, using them to hunt, feed, mate, and protect themselves from prey. But as climate change causes world temperatures to rise, these floating homes are growing scarcer.

In the end, it's thanks to the changing seasons that water transforms the world around us in exciting and surprising ways.

SOME CRATERS ON MARS WERE POSSIBLY CREATED BY SNOWMELT FROM AN ANCIENT GLACIER.

YOU CAN SWIM IN GREAT SAND DUNES NATIONAL PARK, U.S.A., WHEN SNOWMELT CREATES A WIDE STREAM EVERY SUMMER.

A scuba diver in Green Lake, Austria

AXOLOTL ≫

This salamander, found only in the lake complex of Xochimilco (so-chee-MILL-koh) in Mexico City, Mexico, is both adorable and adaptable! Axolotls can regrow almost any body part—feet, legs, tail, jaws, spinal cord—even bits of their heart and brain.

≪ SEA SPIDER

This large, eight-legged creature lives in Antarctic waters. Its porous, Swiss-cheese-like skin gives this arachnid amazing temperature-regulating powers. As the spider grows, its skin creates more holes. The more holes it has, the more oxygen it can absorb, which helps the sea spider cool down or warm up.

SEA ANIMAL

LEAFY SEA DRAGON ≫

A king of camouflage, this relative of the sea-horse uses its luscious leafy exterior to blend into its surroundings, and is able to change colors to match seagrass, kelp, and colorful coral.

SEA ANGEL »

The glowing orange organs of the sea angel are easily visible through their translucent skin. That's if you can even spot this teeny-tiny sea slug in the first place: It's only one to two inches (2.5 to 5 cm) in size.

« SPANISH SHAWL NUDIBRANCH

This purple-and-orange sea slug is an eye-catcher, rhythmically propelling itself through the water. But its vibrant colors warn potential predators that it's poisonous. Not only is it unaffected by a jellyfish sting, it also preys on these creatures, storing their venom to use for its own protection.

ODDITIES

Curious creatures figure out surprising and inspiring ways to survive and thrive in a vast underwater world.

BLUE TANG

A favorite blue fish that likes to keep swimming in packs is surprisingly born yellow! It also hides a secret: When threatened, it extends a knife-sharp, toxin-filled bone from its spine to puncture predators. »

« RED PAPER LANTERN JELLYFISH

Is that a red brain trapped inside an astronaut helmet? Nope, it's a jellyfish! This gelatinous sea creature can squish its inner red layer down like a paper lantern and then puff it back up—an action that helps it swim.

135

SHARK SUPERPOWERS

Sharks exist in a **HUGE VARIETY** of shapes and sizes, each with its own **MIND-BOGGLING SKILLS.** Take a bite out of these **JAW-SOME** shark facts!

A **GREAT HAMMERHEAD SHARK** uses its **WIDE HEAD** to **PIN ITS PREY** to the bottom of the seafloor.

The thresher shark can **WHIP ITS TAIL** at an average **SPEED OF 30 MILES AN HOUR** (48 km/h) to stun its prey.

With more teeth than most sharks, the snakelike **FRILLED SHARK** has **300 TEETH** set in **25 ROWS.**

WHALE SHARKS have powerfully protective skin. At up to **FOUR INCHES** (10 cm) thick, it's the **THICKEST SKIN OF ANY LAND OR SEA ANIMAL.**

A goblin shark can **SHOOT ITS JAW FORWARD** three inches (8 cm) in a single second to **SNAG ITS PREY.**

Because the great white shark doesn't have eyelids, **IT ROLLS ITS EYES TO THE BACK OF ITS HEAD TO PROTECT THEM WHEN THREATENED.**

The dwarf **LANTERNSHARK** not only is the smallest known shark—it can fit in your hand—but also has **A BELLY THAT GLOWS IN THE DARK,** attracting prey in deep water.

137

Ocean
EXPLORATION

WHETHER MANNED OR ROBOTIC, SUBMERSIBLES are the ultimate tool in underwater exploration, helping humans solve some of the deep blue's greatest mysteries. With their help, we can discover new species and habitats, or relocate pieces of history once thought forever lost, like shipwrecks, ancient artifacts, and even lost cities.

Only **5 percent** of the ocean has been **explored.**

The *Titanic* sank in 1912 and wasn't discovered on the seafloor until more than **70 years** later.

12 people have walked on the moon, but only **4** have been to the deepest part of our planet's ocean.

The Silfra fissure in Thingvellir National Park, Iceland, is the only place in the world where you can **snorkel** in a crack between **2 tectonic plates.**

Zealandia, a potential new continent discovered beneath New Zealand, spans **1.9 million square miles** (4.9 million sq km)—roughly the size of India.

Scientists discovered a huge underwater river along the bottom of the Black Sea that is up to **115 feet** (35 m) deep in some places and has rapids and waterfalls.

More than **3,300 years old,** the Uluburun shipwreck off the southwestern coast of Turkey left behind a bounty of artifacts and treasure and is one of the oldest shipwrecks ever discovered.

The Mariana snailfish is the deepest-dwelling fish, living **26,000 feet** (8,000 m) underwater.

Zhemchug Canyon lies underwater in the Bering Sea, and is one of the largest canyons in the world, **2,500 feet** (760 m) deeper than the Grand Canyon.

At **5,000 years old,** the ancient Greek village of Pavlopetri is the oldest sunken city discovered, found **13 feet** (4 m) underwater.

Which Wonder **WOULD YOU CHOOSE?**

LAKE BAIKAL vs.
DEAD SEA

Explore underwater canyons or chill out and float—
at the end of the day, it's up to you to decide into
which watery wonder you'd rather wade!

LAKE BAIKAL
Where: Russia

Standing on the shore of Lake Baikal, in Russia, you
might think you're looking at the ocean. At more than
a mile (1.6 km) deep, Lake Baikal is the deepest lake
on Earth. It's also the oldest—scientists estimate it's
25 million years old! Beneath its crystal blue waters are
mossy canyon cliffs, deep crevices, tunnels, and caves.
A surprise waits at the bottom—a world full of lush
green fauna that resembles a cacti and succulent garden. This divers' delight is home to more than 2,500
species of animals and plants, two-thirds of which are
unique to Lake Baikal, including the adorable Baikal
seal—the planet's only freshwater seal.

Lake Baikal holds about 20 percent of the world's fresh surface water.

Lake Baikal has 27 islands; when the lake freezes in the winter, people drive cars on the ice to travel between islands.

Some geo-physicists think Lake Baikal could be an ocean in the making, as it con-tinues to grow by 0.4 to 0.8 inch (1 to 2 cm) a year.

Lake Baikal's coast-line is 1,300 miles (2,100 km) long—that's nearly as long as the coastline of Oregon, U.S.A.

Baikal seals use their sharp claws to carve breathing holes in the thick ice, which can be up to 6.5 feet (2 m) deep.

THE DEAD SEA
Where: Between Israel and Jordan

No need for a giant inflatable in the Dead Sea. With as much as nine times more salt than the ocean, the water is denser than the human body, allowing for easy floating. In fact, swimming in the Dead Sea, which is located between Israel and Jordan, is almost impossible. Once in the water, you can feel your body getting lighter and the water around you getting springier, like gelatin. What feels like magic is just science at its best! So sit back, relax, and enjoy. But no cannonballs, or you might get tiny scrapes from salt crystals. And don't open your eyes underwater—the salt will make them burn for an hour!

The salt is acclaimed for its healing properties.

The Dead Sea Scrolls, ancient religious writings dating back to the third century B.C., were found in 11 caves nearby in the 1940s and '50s.

The water in the Dead Sea mixes with the mineral-rich soil, creating a mud mask that leaves skin feeling silky and smooth.

The Dead Sea is the lowest point on Earth's land surface.

Originally thought to hold no life—hence the name Dead Sea—scientists have recently found microbial life on the seafloor.

141

More EPIC ➤ SWIMMING HOLES

◀ **RÍO CELESTE**
Where: Guanacaste Province, Costa Rica
This stunning blue swimming hole has a waterfall and neighboring hot springs.

ANCIENT LAVA TUBES FUNNEL OCEAN WATER TO THE TO-SUA TRENCH, CREATING A BEAUTIFUL NATURAL SWIMMING HOLE.

WHAT FIERY EXPLOSION MADE SUCH A SPLASH?

On the island of Upolu, Samoa, a giant swimming hole sits in the hardened lava fields of a volcano. The lush oasis was created when the volcano erupted, causing portions of the island to collapse, including where the To-Sua ocean trench now sits. Water is funneled into the hole by tunnels that were created by flowing lava long ago.

Visitors enter the sparkling emerald water by cliff jumping or climbing down a tall ladder. Once in the swimming hole, it's hard to believe the surrounding walls covered in vibrant plants and hanging vines are cooled remnants of fiery lava. Tucked below a curtain of vines is a shallow entrance to an underwater cave—a hidden reminder of the trench's fiery beginnings.

SELJAVALLALAUG
Where: Iceland
Hot-spring water from a glacier-topped volcano trickles down to form this pool.

EMMA GORGE
Where: Kimberley, Australia
Enjoy a swim between towering rock walls.

SECRETIVE SEA WOLVES

Imagine boating over open ocean water. You might expect to see whales, sharks, and seals. But what about wolves? Though rare to spot, the coastal wolf lives off the coast of British Columbia, Canada, and these adaptable animals count on the ocean to survive. We still have much to learn about these fascinating creatures.

They can SWIM up to 7.5 miles (12 km) across the water to different islands off the coast.

90 percent of their diet is from the ocean—they'll even HUNT SEALS and SEA LIONS.

They have DISTINCT DNA that sets them apart from their inland cousins.

Prevalent in the GREAT BEAR RAINFOREST of British Columbia, they live alongside grizzly bears, black bears, and spirit bears.

They are also referred to as "RAIN WOLVES" because they hunt where the rainforest meets the ocean.

Coastal wolf cubs play TUG-OF-WAR with kelp.

This unique species is in danger: There are NO HUNTING LAWS TO PROTECT THEM and logging businesses tear down rainforest trees.

Swimming in OPEN WATER is dangerous for the wolves—they must swim slowly and not make any sudden movements, or they could be an ocean animal's next meal.

Coastal wolves are approximately 20 PERCENT SMALLER than other wolves.

More Unexpected UNDERWATER ANIMALS

◀ CORAL REEF SNAKE
Where: Western Pacific Ocean
This venomous snake has developed a paddlelike tail that helps it swim through crevices in coral reefs as it hunts for food.

▼ DIVING BELL SPIDER
Where: Europe, Siberia
This is the only spider known to live its entire life underwater.

◀ FLYING FISH
Where: Atlantic, Pacific, and Indian Oceans
The flying fish can soar out of the water at more than 35 miles an hour (56 km/h) and glide up to 650 feet (200 m).

▼ PLATYPUS
Where: Australia
A platypus can sense electrical signals from its prey and is the only mammal that lays eggs.

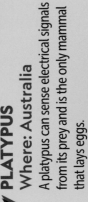

BARNACLES

These crustaceans will stick in your mind. Barnacles are famous for producing a fast-acting cement that allows them to attach to surfaces. This substance is one of the most powerful glues in nature. In fact, scientists are trying to replicate it for human use.

SURFGRASS

Tide pools aren't home to just animals. They also support plants. Surfgrass is one plant that grows in certain tide pools. Some species can grow pretty long. Torrey's surfgrass, which flourishes along the western coast of North America, can stretch to 10 feet (3 m).

Tide pools are pools of salt water left behind when the tide rolls out.

TIDE POOL

SEA STARS

The sea star is a well-known animal—but it still has some surprises. For instance, sea stars don't have blood. Instead, seawater courses through their bodies! This liquid enters through a small opening. The seawater is able to pump nutrients through the sea stars.

SEA URCHIN »

A sea urchin sports supersharp spines over most of its body. But even with this built-in defense system, it still faces predators like fish. Luckily, this creature is a master of disguise. When threatened, it camouflages itself by covering its body with shells and seaweed.

« CHITON

Related to snails and slugs, the chiton spends its days crawling along rocks and munching on algae. This animal may win the prize for weirdest eyes. Most animal eyes are made of proteins. The chiton's peepers are made of aragonite, a type of mineral that can be found in some rocks!

PARTY

The animals and plants in and around tide pools make these spots on the shore super festive!

SEA ANEMONES »

With their cylinder-shaped bodies and masses of tentacles, sea anemones resemble lovely aquatic flowers. But beware: These critters can be toxic. They use their tentacles to inject passing prey with venom, then guide the helpless prey into their mouths.

«

CRABS

Many crabs live around tidal pools. The purple shore crab can be found under rocks and seaweed in these areas. These two-inch (5-cm)-wide critters can produce an impressive amount of offspring. Females can lay clutches of more than 30,000 eggs at a time!

MEXICO'S YUCATAN PENINSULA HAS THOUSANDS OF UNDERWATER CAVERNS CALLED CENOTES, SOME OF WHICH CONTAIN THE **REMAINS** OF ANCIENT HUMANS.

A cenote in the Yucatan Peninsula

CENOTE ▶ CRITTERS

CHECK OUT SOME ANIMALS YOU MAY FIND IN AND AROUND CENOTES.

HOW DID THE REMAINS GET HERE?

The cenotes of the Yucatan Peninsula took tens of thousands of years to form. Long ago, parts of the ground were made of soft rock topped with a hard layer of crust. Over time, acidic rainwater seeped into the ground, dissolving areas of soft rock and creating holes. Then, during the last ice age, the crust over many of the holes collapsed, leaving openings. Once the ice age ended, sea levels rose and the holes filled with water.

In recent years, scientists exploring the cenotes made strange discoveries. They found the remains of ancient giant sloths, saber-toothed cats, and even humans! What were these creatures doing in these watery spots? During the ice age, when sea levels were lower, the cenotes were dry. The people and animals may have wandered into the caverns and fallen into pits, where they perished. More remains were added between A.D. 600 and 1100. During this time, the Maya ruled the Yucatan Peninsula and cenotes became sacred places where humans were sacrificed to appease Maya gods.

Scientists aren't done researching cenotes. Thousands of these caves remain unexplored, and they likely hold even more jaw-dropping mysteries to unravel.

MORELET'S CROCODILE
A Morelet's crocodile usually has 66 to 68 teeth.

MESO-AMERICAN SLIDER
This freshwater turtle species lives in large rivers and marshes, coming out of the water to bask on rocks and logs.

MEXICAN BLIND BROTULA
This cave fish uses its sharp sense of smell to find crustaceans and small fish to eat. It is the top predator in Yucatan waters.

RADICAL
RARITIES

Blood-red moon
over Mt. Rainier,
Washington, U.S.A.

From blood-red moons and rare blooms to strange weather events and see-through butterflies, our universe contains some incredible rarities. They may not always be easy to spot, but when you glimpse one of these unusual wonders, it's an extra-special occasion! Read on to unearth more about the world's uncommon curiosities.

More EXPLOSIVE > VOLCANO FACTS

> When Indonesia's Krakatoa volcano erupted in 1883, the explosion was heard more than 2,000 miles (3,220 km) away.

LIGHTNING CAN BURST FROM AN ERUPTING VOLCANO.

HOW DO THESE LIGHTNING BOLTS FORM?

You'd expect to see lava shooting from a volcano. Ash, sure. But bolts of lightning? It does occasionally happen! For many years, people were stumped by this phenomenon. Then scientists in Germany created a small plume of gas and ash in their lab to mimic a volcanic eruption. While watching film footage of the experiment, they noticed mini lightning bolts in the plume. By studying these bolts, scientists eventually came to an explanation.

Here's how it works: Lightning may form if an eruption produces a thick plume of ash. Within the volcano, the particles that make up this plume are packed together tightly. As they're belched out, the particles rub against one another. This creates friction, which causes the particles to become electrically charged. Moving up the plume, the positively charged particles begin to separate from the negatively charged ones. If the separation between oppositely charged particles becomes too great, an electric bolt will rip through the plume to connect them. And *boom*, there's your volcanic lightning!

Earth has about 1,500 potentially active volcanoes.

In 2004, the extreme sport of volcano surfing was invented in Nicaragua.

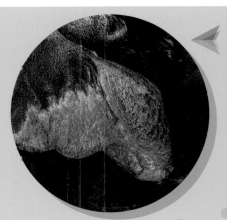
Lava is beyond hot—it can hit 2200°F (1200°C).

153

One-of-a-Kind
CRITTERS

These **UNFORGETTABLE CREATURES**
are found in only **A FEW SPOTS ON EARTH.**

ALL SMILES

The quokka (KWAH-kah) will always greet you with a grin—its mouth is shaped in a smile! Related to kangaroos, these house-cat-size critters mostly inhabit a set of islands off the coast of southwestern Australia. They can often be found lounging around or snacking on plants. These beaming cuties do have a sharp side, though: The animals boast superstrong teeth and claws.

LARGE AND IN CHARGE

Komodo dragons, native to remote parts of Indonesia, are the world's biggest lizards. Some weigh more than 300 pounds (130 kg) and stretch longer than 10 feet (3 m). But that's not all. The Komodo is one of the only venomous lizards on Earth! It delivers a toxic bite to prey, which kills the victim within days. Then the Komodo uses its turbo-charged sense of smell to locate its dinner.

MONKEYING AROUND

Gelada monkeys only inhabit the high mountain meadows of Ethiopia. The furry couch potatoes spend most of their time sitting on their padded rumps. But they also have an adventurous streak—they rock climb! Their short, stumpy fingers are made for scaling cliffs. At night, they crawl down the cliffsides and sleep in groups on rocky ledges.

BEAUTY AND THE BITE

The gooty sapphire tarantula, found only in one region of India, almost seems to sparkle thanks to its bright blue hairs. But beware this flashy gem of a critter—it's extremely venomous. A single bite from the spider can leave a person in pain for more than a week! Like most tarantulas, the gooty sapphire only bites when threatened. Still, you'll want to admire this eye-catching arachnid from afar.

PUCKER UP

Wait, is that fish wearing lipstick? No, but it sure looks that way! Red-lipped batfish only live around the Galápagos Islands. Instead of swimming, they "walk" along the ocean floor on their fins, staying near the ground to blend in with the sandy bottom. Of course, their bright red mouths still stand out. So why do they have them? Scientists think the lips help attract mates.

155

MAGNIFICENT
MULTIPLES

Twins, triplets, quadruplets,

oh my! For humans, giving birth to multiples is **pretty rare.** Identical siblings or fraternal siblings (nonidentical siblings born at the same time) make up only a **small portion of the population.** What's the story behind them? Discover the **many marvels** of multiples.

SEEING DOUBLE

More than 130 million babies are born around the world each year. Only about 3 percent of these are twins. Even fewer are triplets, quadruplets, and so on. These multiples aren't spread out over the globe evenly. Some areas have more multiples than others. In the city of Igbo-Ora in Nigeria, for instance, nearly every household has a set of twins! Scientists still aren't sure why.

Some of the world's multiples are identical. That means they share very similar DNA. Other multiples are fraternal. They share around 50 percent of their DNA, just like siblings born at different times. Identical multiples are much less common than fraternal ones. The chances of having identical twins are three in 1,000. Identical triplets? It's a 20 to 30 in a million happening. Identical quadruplets? There are only about 60 sets worldwide!

HELPING SCIENCE

Multiples are helping scientists learn more about humans in general. Identical multiples may have extremely similar DNA and look alike. However, the siblings are individuals with distinct personalities. They may also have different physical features or medical conditions. Scientists can look at these differences to figure out whether traits or illnesses are inherited or result from the environment.

Twins are also providing some out-of-this-world information! Astronauts Scott Kelly and Mark Kelly are identical twins. From 2015 to 2016, Scott lived aboard the International Space Station. Meanwhile, Mark was back on Earth. Biologists closely monitored the health of each brother during this time. Then they compared the data to see how living in space for a long period affects the human body. The findings could help prepare people for long space voyages, such as trips to Mars.

ANIMALS MULTIPLIED

How common are multiples in the rest of the animal kingdom? For a lot of species, fraternal siblings come along frequently. Many animals, such as dogs and cats, have multiple babies at one time. But identical siblings are exceedingly rare. In fact, humans and one species of armadillo are the only ones known to consistently have identical babies.

Whether they're identical or not, multiples in the animal kingdom are important. Researchers can study the genes of animals that regularly birth multiples to better understand what genes might affect multiples in humans. Plus, these critters can provide double, triple, and sometimes quadruple the cuteness. Now that's magnificence multiplied!

MIRROR TWINS ARE ASYMMETRICAL IDENTICAL TWINS— FOR INSTANCE, ONE SIBLING CAN BE RIGHT-HANDED AND THE OTHER LEFT-HANDED.

Armadillos

Astronauts Mark Kelly and Scott Kelly

IDENTICAL SIBLINGS HAVE DIFFERENT FINGERPRINTS.

SEE-THROUGH SENSATION

It's easy to see why the glass-winged butterfly is cool. Unlike most butterflies, which have colorful wing tissue, this butterfly has transparent wings! Get the facts on this see-through flier.

The butterfly's wings are serving as inspiration for ANTIREFLECTIVE TECHNOLOGY. Such technology could be used on digital screens to cut down on glare from the sun.

The butterfly's CLEAR WING TISSUE doesn't absorb much light. And MICROSCOPIC STRUCTURES on the wings are arranged in such a way that they DON'T REFLECT LIGHT. So light just zips right through the insect's wings. This is what makes them transparent.

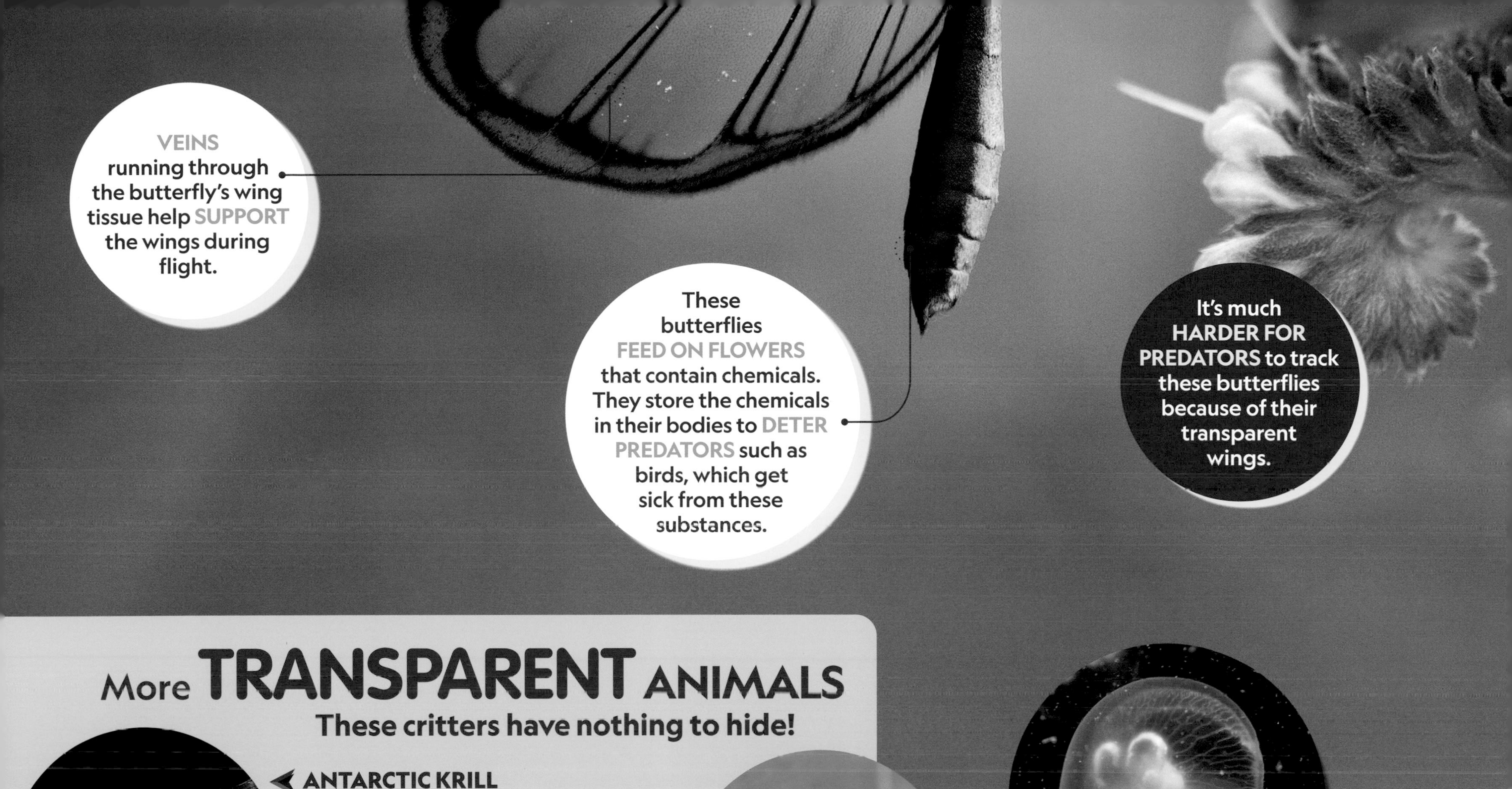

It's much HARDER FOR PREDATORS to track these butterflies because of their transparent wings.

These butterflies FEED ON FLOWERS that contain chemicals. They store the chemicals in their bodies to DETER PREDATORS such as birds, which get sick from these substances.

VEINS running through the butterfly's wing tissue help SUPPORT the wings during flight.

More **TRANSPARENT** ANIMALS
These critters have nothing to hide!

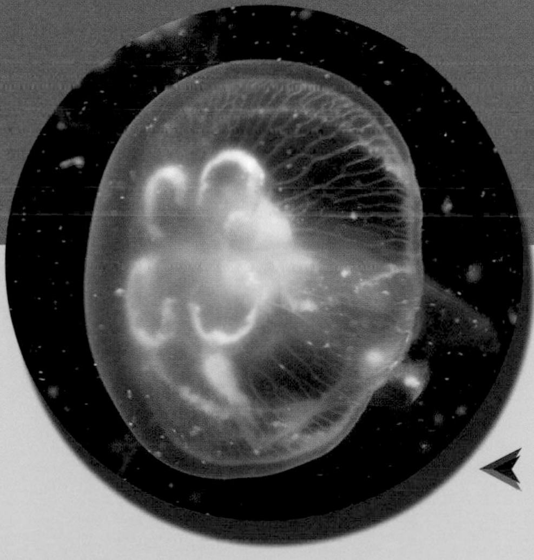

MOON JELLY

TORTOISESHELL BEETLE

GLASS FROG

ANTARCTIC KRILL

159

PENITENTES

On some mountain glaciers, the sun can turn ice immediately into water vapor, rather than melting it first. This process happens faster in some spots than in others. This creates dips where the ice turned to water vapor and nieves penitentes, or spikes, where it remained intact.

WACKY

FIRE WHIRLS »

Fire whirls happen on days when high temperatures combine with heated air from wildfires. This results in a rotating column of hot air and gases. As the spinning air speeds up, it pulls in ashes and flames from the fire, creating a blazing whirl.

« MOONBOWS

Moonbows form when moonlight enters water droplets in the air at a certain angle. The light is bent and reflected back out. As it leaves the droplets, the light is then divided into different colors, creating the nighttime rainbow.

GREEN CLOUDS

Before a hailstorm, the cloudy sky can sometimes turn green. Though some people originally thought the sky was reflecting grass, experts disproved that idea. It's more likely that thunderclouds filter out all the colors that make up light except for green.

WATERMELON SNOW

When snow at high altitudes melts a bit during spring and summer, green algae that thrived in the frigid flakes are suddenly exposed to the sun. The algae produce a natural sunscreen that turns the snow a watermelon pink!

WEATHER

These odd weather events will blow your mind!

SPRITES

Electrical bursts known as sprites can occur 50 miles (80 km) above Earth's surface over very active thunderstorms. Sprites glow red due to the presence of nitrogen gas and only last a few milliseconds before they're gone in a flash.

SUN DOGS

On rare occasions, patches of light called sun dogs shine on either side of the sun. They form when sunlight streams through hexagon-shaped ice crystals at the right angle. The crystals bend the rays in such a way that it creates the illusion of the two bright orbs.

Rare OBJECTS

SOME OBJECTS ARE SO OUT OF THE ORDINARY, THEY GET A FAN FOLLOWING. Unusual gems, stamps with mistakes, famous artwork—such items draw admirers and collectors. Sometimes they're placed in museums for all to see. And sometimes they become worth a pretty penny! Here are some figures behind amazingly rare doodads and one-of-a-kind objects.

Known as the Olympic Australis, the largest and most valuable opal, a rough gem, is **17,000 carats** and weighs **7.6 pounds** (3.45 kg).

Built in 1741, a rare violin from Italy was priced at **$18 million.**

At **more than 600 years old,** the one-of-a-kind Palatine Crown is the oldest surviving crown of England.

A stamp known as an Inverted Jenny, which was accidentally printed with an upside-down plane, sold at auction for **more than $1 million.**

A collector **paid $454,000** for a **12-cent** copy of *Amazing Fantasy* **no. 15,** the first comic book to feature Spider-Man.

Only **5 Aston Martin DBR1s** were ever built, making the car worth an estimated **$22.5 million.**

Tiny moon rocks brought back to Earth from a 1970 space mission were sold for **$855,000.**

Every day, **about 30,000 people** visit the "Mona Lisa" painting at the Louvre in Paris, France.

163

Nature TAKEOVER

Sometimes, **NATURE FINDS A WAY** to really **SHOW US WHO'S BOSS.**

PLANT POWER
Where: Shengshan Island, China

In the 1990s, families living on one small island off eastern China began moving to the mainland for jobs. Within about a decade, the village became a ghost town. Without anyone to cut down the island's plants, the greenery began to grow over all the buildings. Now the abandoned village has become a draw for tourists who want to gawk at this unique green explosion.

ICED OUT
Where: Ohio, U.S.A.

Occasionally in winter, the West Pierhead Lighthouse transforms into an unusual ice palace. When temperatures drop really low, freezing waves and spray from nearby Lake Erie can coat the building in layer upon layer of ice. Sometimes even the light beam is blocked out. And the building's icy shell can remain for months on end. At least all this ice looks nice!

LAND OF SAND
Where: Al Madam, United Arab Emirates
The abandoned village of Al Madam has an uncommon intruder—it's been completely invaded by desert sand! According to local legend, supernatural creatures called jinns forced the villagers of Al Madam to flee their town. What may have really driven people away were winds that pushed sand into the dwellings. Either way, this town turned sandbox is pretty striking.

TREES TAKE CHARGE
Where: Angkor, Cambodia
The temple of Ta Prohm was built in 1186 in Angkor, the capital of the wealthy Khmer Empire. After being abandoned centuries later, tree roots and vines called strangler figs crawled all over the building. In the 20th century, French explorers came across the temple ruins, which peeked out from the tangle of roots and vines. The temple had become a rare sight—a man-made structure that had merged almost completely with nature.

DROWNED TOWN
Where: Villa Epecuén, Argentina
In 1985, floodwater busted through a dam near Villa Epecuén. The water level in the village rose slowly, allowing the residents to flee unharmed. Eventually, the entire abandoned village was submerged in 33 feet (10 m) of water. About 25 years after the flooding began, the waters receded, revealing parts of the soaked village. Today, buildings, roads, and trees are visible. You can even still see the layout of the town from above. But this soggy spot is still a water world.

165

More AMAZING ▷ EYES

THESE UNFORGETTABLE
EYES REALLY STICK OUT!

◁ DRAGONFLY

CRAB ▷

BLUE-EYED BLACK LEMURS ARE ONE OF THE ONLY PRIMATES BESIDES HUMANS TO HAVE BLUE EYES.

WHAT'S WITH THEIR STARTLING PEEPERS?

More than 300 primate species live in the world, and most only have brown or gold eyes. With eye color ranging from brown to green to blue, humans are an exception. So are blue-eyed black lemurs. These small primates are native to the rainforests of Madagascar, an island nation off Africa. Unlike humans, male and female blue-eyed black lemurs only have bright turquoise irises.

Scientists know why human eye color is sometimes blue. Until at least 6,000 years ago, all humans had brown eyes. Then a mutation, or change, to a gene called *HERC2* affected another gene called *OCA2*. This led to some people having blue, green, or hazel eyes. Scientists wondered if the same genes were responsible for the lemur's baby blues. They ran tests but found out that they weren't in fact the cause. Experts continue to try to crack the mystery of the lemur's rare eye color.

Unfortunately, blue-eyed black lemurs are rare for another reason: They're critically endangered, with fewer than 1,000 estimated to be remaining in the wild. However, conservationists are working hard to protect them.

HAMMERHEAD SHARK

GOAT

LEAF-TAILED GECKO

7 JAW-DROPPING FACTS ABOUT …

UNCOMMON EVENTS

Certain events are **SO INFREQUENT,** they make an **EXTRA-STRONG IMPRESSION** when they finally do occur. Check out some **UNCOMMON HAPPENINGS** that are … wait for it … **PRETTY AMAZING.**

The **QUEEN OF THE ANDES** plant can take a **CENTURY TO BLOOM.**

SWEET CHERRY TREES can take more than **FIVE YEARS TO YIELD FRUIT.**

Periodical **CICADAS HIBERNATE FOR 13 TO 17 YEARS,** then emerge from underground over a two-week period.

The **TAI PING CHING JIU** religious **FESTIVAL** takes place **ONCE A DECADE** on the outskirts of Hong Kong.

DERECHOS—fast-moving **CLUSTERS OF THUNDERSTORMS** with superstrong **WINDS**—occur about **ONCE A YEAR.**

HALLEY'S COMET enters Earth's vicinity **EVERY 75 YEARS** or so.

ABOUT TWICE EVERY THREE YEARS, a total lunar eclipse makes the **MOON** look **BLOOD RED.**

Exceptional
EATS

LIKE RARE FOODS? Then you'll eat this up. Check out this GRUB—and the high prices some people pay for it.

PULE CHEESE
Donkeys only produce a small amount of milk each day. In fact, a cow generates about 30 times the amount of milk a donkey does! So donkey milk isn't usually used to make cheese. But pule cheese from the country of Serbia boasts donkey milk. And people are willing to pay a lot for the dairy product. One pound (0.5 kg) of pule can cost more than $1,000!

MANUKA HONEY
This gooey golden treat is produced by bees that use nectar from the manuka bush, a plant found in New Zealand and Australia. The honey can be made for only a few weeks each year when manuka flowers are in bloom. After the bees make the honey, beekeepers collect and sell it, often for a lot of money. One batch of the rare honey was priced at more than $1,000 a jar.

WHITE TRUFFLES

Truffles are edible fungi, like mushrooms. They grow underground near the roots of certain trees, making them difficult to locate. In fact, people use trained dogs or pigs to sniff out the fungi. Found in just one part of Italy, white truffles are even harder than most to track down. Maybe that's why people have shelled out $2,000 for just one pound (0.5 kg) of this delicacy!

DENSUKE WATERMELON

In Japan, you can find watermelons that resemble bowling balls! Known as Densuke watermelons, these fruits are smooth with an almost black rind. They're grown on the island of Hokkaido. After being harvested, the watermelons are auctioned off to the highest bidder. And here's a juicy detail: A person once paid $6,100 for one of the melons.

La Bonnotte potatoes have a lemony flavor.

LA BONNOTTE POTATOES

These taters come from an island off France. Farmers plant small batches of them in the island's sandy soil. The spuds that sprout are too fragile to be collected with a machine, so each must be handpicked. Because of the difficulty in cultivating the vegetable, each pound (0.5 kg) can sell for hundreds of dollars. That's no small potatoes!

TERRIFIC
TECHNOLOGY
AND INSPIRING INVENTIONS

Holographic horses at the Circus Roncalli, Germany

Envisioning the endless possibilities of what the future could hold dates back to ancient times, when our most creative ancestors dared to dream outside of the box. Incredible inventions and smart solutions throughout history continue to pave the way for a fantastic future. Discover the world's game-changing technologies of today, from robots that retrieve sunken treasure to a circus saving the planet one holographic animal at a time.

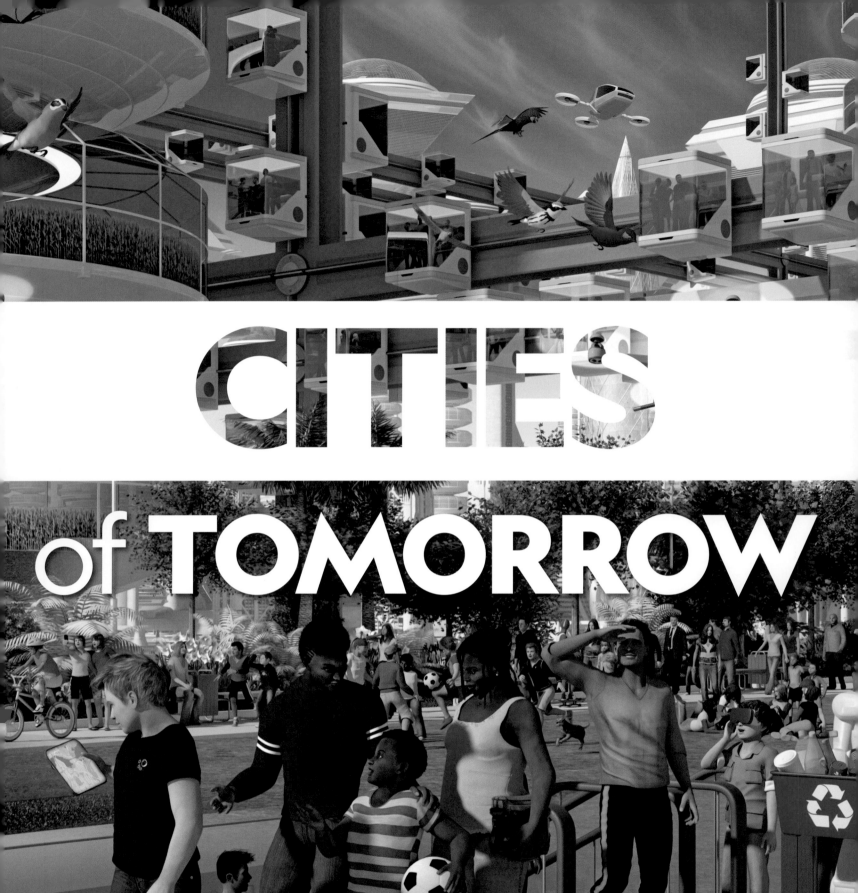

CITIES
of TOMORROW

Scientists and sci-fi lovers alike have imagined a wild world full of **cool technology** that makes our home a more exciting and productive place to live. Dreams of a **new-age city** are becoming the stuff of reality. Take, for instance, the Shard in London, the tallest building in the United Kingdom, with **95 stories.** It is described as a **"vertical city"** with homes, shops, restaurants, and offices. And most notably, it's an **eco-friendly** triumph, as 95 percent of the materials used to construct it were recycled.

SKYSCRAPERS

Many argue that the skyscrapers of the future can't just stand tall looking pretty—like the Shard, they should play a more powerful role in building the community and improving the natural landscape. Trash, believe it or not, is taking the future of skyscraper construction by storm. As trash continues to take up more and more space, scientists are figuring out ways to compact yesterday's sandwich wrappers and milk cartons into literal building blocks for skyscrapers.

ARTIFICIAL ISLANDS

Beyond just single buildings, even bigger ideas are in the works. Denmark plans to finish nine artificial islands by 2040. When cities build roads, buildings, bridges, and such, they dig up a lot of soil to make room for the new structures. So where does that excess soil go? It's treated like garbage, taking up loads of space in a landfill. To help this dirty issue, Copenhagen plans to recycle about 900 million cubic feet (26 million m³) of excess soil to create the new islands. Moreover, the islands will be home to eco-driven businesses, wind turbines used to produce energy, parks for outdoor activities, a facility that turns waste into energy, and protected wildlife habitats.

CLOUD CITIES AND BEYOND

While we perfect cities on the ground, the dream of cities in the sky is also starting to take shape, not just on Earth, but on other planets. Scientists plan to take a closer look at Venus as a backup home for humans, but there is one problem—the land on Venus is so hot it destroys nearly any type of material that comes into contact with it. So what's there to do? Look up to the clouds. Scientists believe that the atmosphere 30 miles (50 km) above the surface of Venus is very similar to Earth's, meaning humans could potentially survive there. But before humans can create a city in the clouds, researchers plan to first send robots to study the atmosphere so we can further understand its potential effects.

These are just a few of the ways that humans are reimagining cities. Soon, it'll be up, up, and away as we take off into the future!

A TOWN IN POLAND HAS SOLAR-POWERED GLOW-IN-THE-DARK BIKE PATHS, MAKING STREETS SAFER FOR BICYCLISTS AT NIGHT.

TO LESSEN THE IMPACT OF PLASTIC WASTE ON EARTH, SCIENTISTS ARE STUDYING PLASTIC-EATING CATERPILLARS.

Aerial photograph of skyscrapers in Shanghai, China

Robot
ROUNDUP

Humans are coming up with a slew of **RAD ROBOTS** that will transform our planet, from tiny **FLYING BOTS** to cuddly **BIONIC CRITTERS** to **CYBORG** pioneers.

AIBO ROBOT DOG

Woof-woof! Ready for a new-age man's best friend? Aibo is an adorable robotic dog equipped with multiple sensors and cameras on its body to help it interact with its owners. Like RoboBee, this barking buddy was created by studying real dogs. Because of its special artificial intelligence program, it can get to know its owners by learning what certain actions and facial expressions mean. It understands popular commands like "sit" and "high-five" and unique ones like "dance" and "sing." You can even cuddle with Aibo—it recognizes when you're petting it. As Aibo's creators strive to make it as close to a real pet pooch as paw-ssible, more and more features continue to roll out. Now there's even an app in which you can feed Aibo food or potty train it—but don't worry, nothing really comes out of Aibo—it's all virtual!

Aibo can locate the source of a sound and turn its head in the direction of a person's voice.

ROBOBEE X-WING

The race to make the smallest insect-size flying robot is on! Meet the RoboBee X-Wing—the lightest robot to fly without a tether. No bigger than a paper clip, it is solar-powered with two pairs of wings that flap more than 120 times a second! Scientists studied real flying insects to create materials light enough to help this bee soar. For instance, RoboBee X-Wing has wings to help it fly instead of a propeller because wings can make more precise movements, are much quieter, and are safer for the robot and its surroundings. It's a huge step toward an exciting future, in which scientists believe teeny-tiny robots will complete intricate surgeries, explore hard-to-reach planets, and find survivors in natural disasters.

ROBO-DIVER

Here's one mermaid that's for real. Because many places underwater are extremely difficult for humans to reach, a group of scientists set out to build a robot that could do the impossible. OceanOne slightly resembles a mermaid, with the head, arms, and torso of a human, and a chunky fish tail made of batteries, thrusters, and computers. It has humanlike vision and an artificial "brain," but its most important feature is its sensor-filled hands. These allow scientists to not only see what it's seeing underwater, but feel what it's feeling! For OceanOne's first adventure, it successfully retrieved an artifact from a ship that sank to the bottom of the Mediterranean Sea in 1664. The groundbreaking maneuverability and flexibility of OceanOne brought history to shore.

7 JAW-DROPPING **FACTS** ABOUT …

BIONIC ANIMALS

These **BREATHTAKING BIONIC** animals are **BREAKING BARRIERS.**

Scientists have **TRAINED MOTHS** to **CONTROL ROBOTIC VEHICLES** by moving their feet over a device that controls the cars.

After a boat struck a **SEA TURTLE** and **BROKE ITS SHELL,** students used **3D PRINTING** to make a **NEW ONE.** ▼

It took Mosha the **ASIAN ELEPHANT** just 12 hours to learn how to walk on her **PROSTHETIC LEG,** which was **ONE OF THE LARGEST PROSTHETICS EVER** made.

Winter the **DOLPHIN** received a **PROSTHETIC TAIL** that allowed her to **LEAP 10 FEET** (3 m) out of the water!

The size of **HUMAN HANDS,** **BionicANTs** can communicate with one another and work together to get a task done like real ants do.

NAKI'O LOST ALL FOUR PAWS DUE TO FROSTBITE when he was a puppy, but with lots of love and support, he soon became the **FIRST DOG IN THE WORLD** to wear **FOUR PROSTHETIC LEGS.**

In an ongoing study, scientists have implanted **BRAIN SENSORS IN GRASSHOPPERS** to create **CYBORG BUGS** that can **SNIFF OUT EXPLOSIVES** with their antennae.

The FUTURE OF > HOLOGRAMS

We'll be able to attend concerts featuring life-like hologram versions of popular singers who have passed away.

A CIRCUS IN GERMANY PERFORMS WITH HOLOGRAPHIC ANIMALS INSTEAD OF LIVE ONES.

HOW DOES THIS DIGITAL DAZZLE WORK?

You won't see any live animals under this big top. The Circus Roncalli in Germany once performed with real animals, but to address concerns with their health and safety, the circus replaced them with animal holograms. The circus is still set up in a traditional round theater with an audience on all sides, but animals zap into view on center stage like a magic trick, including a large elephant, a goldfish the size of a zebra, and horses that stampede around the circus ring. These 3D projections interact with the ringmaster and the rest of the performers, just as their flesh-and-fur counterparts would.

Fifteen 3D designers and engineers helped bring the astounding performance of laser beams to life. The digital animals can be projected much larger than they are in reality, which makes for an awe-worthy show! And Circus Roncalli has also included a robotic acrobat that can perform alongside a human partner.

Doctors will study holographic organs to better understand the human body.

Holograms of real authors will be able to read their books to listeners.

To better communicate around the world, humans will have identical hologram avatars that can speak other languages for them.

Symphony of THE SEAS

THE SYMPHONY OF THE SEAS WAS THE WORLD'S LARGEST CRUISE SHIP when it was built, and boasts an astounding number of features—a laser tag arena, water parks, rock-climbing walls, mini-golf, an ice-skating rink, and even a robotic waiter that serves drinks. Let's set sail and stack up its exciting stats.

The Aqua Theater

The ship has two **43-foot (13-m)-tall** rock-climbing walls.

There are **2,200** crew members.

It is **1,188 feet (362 m)** long.

Splashaway Bay aqua park

It has **24** water features, including swimming pools, whirlpools, surf simulators, and waterslides.

Robotic waiter

Ice-skating rink

It contains **2,759** guest rooms.

The cost of building the *Symphony* was **$1.35 billion.**

4,700 people helped build the *Symphony*.

There is a slide called the Ultimate Abyss on board, which has a **92-foot (28-m)** drop.

A zip line on the **9th** deck spans **82 feet (25 m).**

Mini-golf course

ECO-FRIENDLY CITIES

Big cities around the world are setting new standards for clean living, making everyday life better for residents. See what cool steps they're taking to transform their city, and the world, into a better place!

Hot Springs Power
Where: Reykjavík, Iceland

This chilly city sits on top of a surprising secret—hot springs! Also known as geothermal wells, these natural pools of warm mineral water create steam that Reykjavík uses to generate electricity. And it's not just a little electricity—there's enough to power the entire city. In fact, unlike any other city in the world, only 0.1 percent of Iceland's total electricity is produced from fossil fuels like oil and coal.

Miles of Bikeways
Where: Portland, Oregon, U.S.A.

The people of Portland were born to ride, and it's making a huge difference! Known as the bike capital of the United States, the area has more than 380 miles (610 km) of bikeways, and more than 25 percent of the city's residents use bikes or public transportation, or carpool. Thanks to this *wheely* big effort, Portland significantly lowered its carbon emissions. Plus, the League of American Bicyclists awarded Portland the highest rating—platinum—for being a bicycle-friendly community.

Solar Supertrees
Where: Singapore

Giant "supertrees" that light up at night are foliage worth fawning over. These 18 steel supertrees stand between 80 and 160 feet (25 and 50 m) tall in an area of Singapore known as Gardens by the Bay. Considered vertical gardens, these soaring structures feature tropical flowers and ferns that climb all the way up their "trunk" and branch out at the top. In addition to being pieces of environmental art, they also collect rainwater and generate solar power for this Asian city-state.

Water-Saving Superheroes

Where: Cape Town, South Africa

To overcome a devastating drought, Cape Town pulled off a water-saving feat of superhero standards—it reduced its water usage by nearly 60 percent within three years. Big industries and brave individuals stepped up to the plate to embrace this big change: A restaurant designed a menu with meals that use minimal water; a hotel installed a filtration system that converts ocean water to purified drinking water; and individuals tracked their water use with a special website. Helpful tips from the local government also included flushing the toilet only once a day, and turning the shower off when applying shampoo and soap.

Radical Rooftop

Where: San Francisco, California, U.S.A.

Rising high in the San Francisco skyline is the epic Salesforce Tower, an environmental force to be reckoned with. At 1,070 feet (326 m) tall, it features a game-changing rooftop to help offset its own carbon footprint. The rooftop has a park with greenery designed to absorb carbon dioxide produced by its own bus terminal, and houses wind turbines to help power the building. Beyond its rad rooftop, it also has the city's first black-water, aka sewage, recycling system, which saves 7.8 million gallons (29.5 million L) of water each year.

Recycling Rewards

Where: Curitiba, Brazil

Curitiba is full of recycling geniuses! Without a budget for a true recycling program, the city figured out a way to thank its people for joining in on the effort. By bringing their recycling to special waste stations, people are rewarded with everything from bus tickets to help getting to and from work, to food and even schoolbooks. In the end, Curitiba shows that prioritizing the environment can be a tool to strengthen and grow communities.

Marvelous Mud Houses

Where: Accra, Ghana

To provide more housing options in Accra, a team created "rammed houses"—structures made mostly from mud that cost $5,000 for a one-room home. It's a tried-and-tested technique that's been around for centuries—parts of the Great Wall of China were built with rammed earth. Ghana is very hot, but unfortunately air-conditioning systems are not always affordable or eco-friendly. The mud walls serve as natural insulation to keep the houses cool. An added bonus? They're soundproof and keep out insects. Plus, only 5 percent of the mud mixture uses cement, as cement accounts for about 6 to 7 percent of the planet's carbon emissions.

Sun-Soaked Cities

Where: Freiberg, Germany

Two communities in the heart of Germany have been built with super power-saving abilities, so much so that they gave the cities solar-inspired names! Sonnenschiff means "Sun Ship," and Solarsiedlung means "Solar Village." Buildings for businesses and homes have been perfectly designed with flat rooftops made of solar panels that allow the sun to soak in. Between solar-paneled rooftops and materials that balance the buildings' temperature, the buildings are generating four times more power than they use.

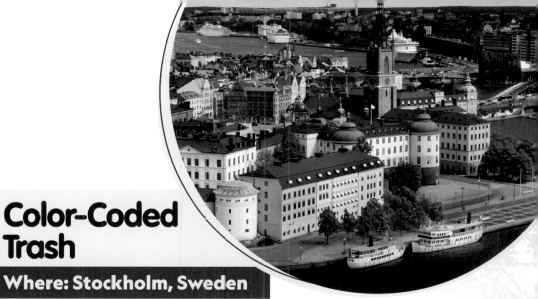

Color-Coded Trash

Where: Stockholm, Sweden

In Sweden, throwing out garbage doesn't have to be a bland and boring chore. The country's special waste management system puts different types of waste in different-colored bags. The bags are then deposited into chutes, where they enter an underground vacuum system. Sensors in the chutes identify the bags' colors and sort them accordingly. This can measure exactly what people are throwing away and reward those who are the greenest.

The Gold Standard

Where: Vancouver, British Columbia, Canada

Building movie theaters, museums, restaurants, malls, theme parks—you name it—takes a heavy toll on the environment, and especially impacts the air we breathe. To ensure we can still enjoy all of our favorite outings, and then some, Vancouver requires that all new buildings meet the Leadership in Energy and Environmental Design (LEED) Gold standard for environmental performance.

AIRPLANE

In 1903, the Wright brothers successfully flew the first powered aircraft at Kill Devil Hills, near Kitty Hawk, North Carolina, U.S.A. Flight technology quickly became every country's obsession, but getting planes to go farther, higher, and carry more weight was a tricky puzzle to solve that took patience and genius.

WHEEL

The wheel is hailed as one of the most fundamental inventions of all time. With a design that hasn't changed in some 6,000 years, wheels gave humans an easy way to transport goods—and people—around the globe. It also inspired hundreds of *spin*-tastic inventions, including clocks and engines.

INVENTIONS

PRINTING PRESS

Though printed materials had been around for ages, it wasn't until the 19th century that books and newspapers could be printed much quicker—and therefore information, knowledge, and education could be more widely available to people around the world.

SMARTPHONES AND APPS

When the first smartphone was released in 1993, it came with only a few basic apps, such as email, a calendar, and a calculator. With apps today that offer everything from food delivery to movie tickets, it's safe to say we've come a long way!

COMPASS

The first compass to help with navigation was made simply of a bowl of water and a floating magnetic needle, dating to 11th-century China.

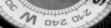

RADIO

In the 19th century when the first radio wave was detected, most people didn't believe wireless transmissions would be useful, let alone even possible. But the discovery paved the way for radio stations, TV stations, cell phones, and loads of other electronics that are far from fictionalized.

THAT ROCKED THE WORLD

These bold inventions of the past were some of the biggest technological game changers.

CARS

The first electric and motorized cars were invented in the mid to late 1800s, and since then it's been off to the races! The two types of cars would compete in efficiency and price for years to come, as they still do today.

SpaceShipTwo is
60 feet
(18.3 m) long—
about the length of a
bowling lane.

SpaceShipTwo can carry
2 pilots and
6 tourists
at a time.

Passengers must do
3 days of
training and
preparation
before their flight.

Once in space,
passengers on
SpaceShipTwo
experience
zero
gravity.

Flights on
SpaceShipTwo will last about
90 minutes,
a few minutes of which
will be spent in space.

Tickets for SpaceShipTwo
are estimated to cost
$250,000.

Space PLANE

WANT TO GO ON AN OUTING THAT'S A LITTLE OUT THERE? Thanks to cutting-edge technology, day trips into space will soon be possible! Several companies are building and testing spaceships for tourists. Virgin Galactic's SpaceShipTwo is one such vehicle. It's designed to take passengers on short flights that will leave Earth's atmosphere. Check out some amazing stats about this spacecraft.

The craft has a **wingspan of 27 feet** (8.3 m).

The craft can travel at **almost 3.5 times the speed of sound.**

More than 600 people reserved spots for the first flights on SpaceShipTwo.

The plan is for **SpaceShipTwo flights to climb 50 miles** (80 km) above Earth's surface.

N202VG

Which Wonder WOULD YOU CHOOSE?
FLYING CAR vs. SPACE ELEVATOR

The future is full of opportunities to reenvision how humans can get around town and take in new sights, from flying cars to an elevator that goes from Earth into space. Decide which wild ride is perfect for you!

A high-rise in Miami, Florida, U.S.A., plans to be the first to have a rooftop specifically for flying cars to take off and land.

Multi-person air taxis could be available as soon as 2025.

While many countries compete for a multi-passenger flying car, Dubai is testing a flying motorbike!

There are at least 15 different flying cars in development.

Flying cars could use an app to initiate takeoff and landing.

FLYING CAR

Imagine buzzing through a city in a flying car, zipping past skyscrapers and passing birds as they breeze by. This fantasy isn't so far-fetched after all, as the biggest names in car and aviation technology race to be the first to develop the best car for the clouds. But you might be a passenger before you're a pilot, as the first flying cars will likely be taxis that can usher around multiple people. There are a lot of kinks to work out still, especially developing batteries that are strong, lightweight, and last a long time—or at least long enough to spell your name in the sky.

SPACE ELEVATOR

We've heard the fantastical stories about elevators that can fly or transport you anywhere, but the tale winning over scientists' hearts is that of the elevator to space. The most promising plan yet uses a long cable that starts on Earth and disappears into the clouds like a tall, magical beanstalk. With the press of a button, an elevator car appears, whisking you up, up, up—the stars around you getting brighter and our big blue planet getting smaller. Scientists continue to refine the latest technology, crowning a new era of space tourism that could soon be more than just a fairy tale.

In 1895, Russian scientist Konstantin Tsiolkovsky was the first person to propose the idea of a space elevator.

A material called graphene could be strong enough to anchor the elevator to Earth—it's 200 times stronger than steel.

China hopes to build a space elevator by 2045, and Japan by 2050.

Other than passengers, the space elevator would also take astronauts and cargo into space.

It could rise 60,000 miles (96,560 km) above Earth.

NASA has funded money for research but hasn't confirmed plans to build one.

MIRACULO
MYSTERIES

US

Our planet is riddled with secrets, whether it's ancient structures built by unknown cultures, tales of wild animals that could be real or mythical, or bizarre objects that seem to have appeared out of nowhere. People travel near and far in an attempt to explain the unexplained, but there's still so much we don't know. Journey through time and space to see which strange stories we've solved and which still stump us today.

Moai statues, Easter Island

History's MYSTERIES

The discovery of some of HISTORY'S MOST INTRIGUING MYSTERIES leads to more questions than answers.

At some point the Sphinx may have been covered in vibrant paint; evidence of blue, red, and yellow still exist on it.

SPHINX
Where: Egypt

For thousands of years no one knew who built the massive Sphinx statue near Egypt's Pyramids at Giza. It was built to honor the Egyptian god of the sky, Horus, but recent archaeological excavations found that the Sphinx might also represent Pharaoh Khafre, the namesake and builder of the second largest pyramid. Who had the Sphinx built isn't the only enduring question. Many believe something important was buried underneath it—but what? One legend said the library of the lost city of Atlantis was concealed below it. Archaeologists went looking for it in the 1920s and discovered a secret passageway under the Sphinx, but it led nowhere. Whatever was once there was likely stolen hundreds of years ago, leaving questions still lingering—and leaving little light at the end of this tunnel.

PLAIN OF JARS
Where: Laos

Legend says that these large stone jars might've been cups giants used to sip a celebratory drink after winning an epic battle. Thousands of them are scattered across a grassy plain for miles, some standing 10 feet (3 m) tall and weighing eight tons (7 t). They've been there for nearly 2,000 years, but what are they? Some researchers believe they were used to collect rainwater from monsoons during the dry season. Or something more spiritual may have been in the works—human remains were discovered in a nearby cave. This suggests the jars could have been used as funeral urns. But until the jars spill their secrets, scientists are left confused by these containers.

STONEHENGE
Where: Wiltshire, England, U.K.

No one knows exactly how or why a curious circle of enormous stones—some as heavy as 10 small African elephants—were transported to this site 4,500 years ago. A 12th-century legend claims that giants placed the monument on a mountain in Ireland, and then a wizard named Merlin magically moved the stone circle to England. But researchers are digging deep to find the truth. Near the site, they discovered bones from the auroch—a species of cattle twice the size of a modern-day bull. These bones date back to 7500 B.C. and were found with thousands of hunting tools, meaning the area was likely used as a hunting ground. It's possible that descendants of these settlers assembled the mysterious stone ring, but for now, Stonehenge's story still isn't written in stone.

7 JAW-DROPPING **FACTS** ABOUT ...

VANISHED
SOCIETIES

It's unclear exactly how these societies that existed hundreds or even thousands of years ago **VANISHED**—could it have been a **VOLCANIC ERUPTION, DISEASE, WAR, OR CLIMATE CHANGE?**—but **CLUES** to their cultures remain.

Considered the **FIRST EUROPEAN CIVILIZATION,** the Minoans were known for their **MYTH OF THE MINOTAUR**—a half-man, half-bull creature that lived within an **INTRICATE LABYRINTH.** ▼

THE MAYA—whose descendants live in **CENTRAL AMERICA** and **MEXICO**—invented the **NUMBER ZERO** and **CREATED HUNDREDS OF HIEROGLYPHS** to represent the written language.

The **CUCUTENI-TRYPILLIAN PEOPLE,** who lived circa 6000 B.C. in eastern Europe, **BURNED THEIR ENTIRE VILLAGE EVERY 60 TO 80 YEARS,** relocating and rebuilding the same structures.

One of the most powerful civilizations from the first to eighth centuries A.D., the **AKSUM OF ETHIOPIA** were the **FIRST TO USE COINS AS MONEY.**

The **CAHOKIA CIVILIZATION,** which existed from the A.D. 800s until the 14th century **IN MODERN-DAY ILLINOIS,** U.S.A., built a city around **120 GRASSY MOUNDS** that can still be seen today.

More than **100 ENGLISH SETTLERS** arrived in modern-day North Carolina, U.S.A., in 1587, but **BY 1590 THEY HAD DISAPPEARED,** leaving behind only the mysterious word "Croatoan" carved into a fence post.

The Indus Valley civilization—one of the **OLDEST AND LARGEST IN THE WORLD**—disappeared from parts of **MODERN-DAY INDIA AND THE MIDDLE EAST** around 1700 B.C., after flourishing for 2,000 years.

CHIMERA

This infamous monster of Greek mythology has the head of a lion, the body of a goat, and a serpent's tail. Chimera was known for breathing fire and terrorizing humans until the hero Bellerophon brought it down while riding a Pegasus—a winged, flying horse.

MERMAIDS

Half human and half fish, the elusive mermaid is often portrayed as charming and serene, but this isn't always the case. Stories throughout history have also portrayed mermaids as dangerous, drowning sailors or calling upon storms to destroy boats.

MYTHICAL

YETI

The yeti, also known as the Abominable Snowman, is part ape, part human—and all parts scary! It sports white fur that blends into the snowy Himalayan mountains of Asia. The only traces it leaves are notoriously ginormous footprints.

LOCH NESS MONSTER

Researchers compare Nessie's likeness to a plesiosaur—an extinct, long-necked marine dinosaur. The monster is said to swim the waters of Loch (Lake) Ness in Scotland, with the first recorded sighting dating back nearly 1,500 years, but there is still no proof it exists.

KRAKEN

This tentacled sea beast is most often likened to an enormous squid—a sailor's worst nightmare. The kraken is said to wrap its tentacles around giant ships and steal them down into the sea, leaving behind a deathly whirlpool to suck down any stragglers.

◀◀ WEREWOLVES

Most werewolves are said to transform only during a full moon, when their thirst for blood becomes uncontrollable. They feed on humans and animals until the sun rises and they turn back into humans. Legend says one of the few ways to kill a werewolf is to burn it.

CREATURES

Many fantastical beasts and magical creatures were once thought to be real.

DRAGONS

This enormous serpentlike creature has an astounding history, with stories dating back thousands of years. In Western tradition, dragons have wings and terrorize villages, while in Eastern tradition they don't have wings and are known as peaceful creatures that represent good luck.

STORIES OF UNICORNS WERE LIKELY BASED ON RHINOS AND HORNED WHALES CALLED NARWHALS.

WHAT MAGIC DID THEIR HORNS HOLD?

The legend of the unicorn spans thousands of years, with stories and artwork from around the world. One ancient description characterizes the unicorn as having a black horn three feet (1 m) long and stumpy elephant-like feet, and making a deep bellowing sound. If you're thinking this crude creature couldn't possibly be the graceful, horselike white creature we know today, then you'd be correct! This first description was likely based on the rhinoceros.

In ancient times, stories of the unicorn's magic mystified people. During the Middle Ages (fifth to 15th centuries), horns from rhinos or tusks from narwhals were sold as unicorn horns. Rumor had it that sipping from a "unicorn horn" could protect the drinker from poison—or at the very least cure an upset stomach.

More MYTHOLOGICAL CREATURES

KAPPA
Where: Japan
This scaly child-size creature with a shell was likely based on the Japanese giant salamander.

CHUPACABRA
Where: Mexico
This terrifying creature with sharp jaws was likely based on a coyote with a scaly skin disease.

CYCLOPS
Where: Greece
With a skull sporting a giant hole in the middle, the Cyclops could have been based on *Deinotherium giganteum*, an ancient elephant relative.

EASTER ISLAND

On Easter Island, otherwise known as Rapa Nui, hundreds of oversize faces carved out of volcanic rock stare back at you. When the *moai* statues were first discovered, it was assumed they were just heads without bodies—an eerie sight to behold with nearly 1,000 of them lined up in the grass. But archaeologists found that the statues do have bodies—they're just buried in the ground. No one knows who made them or why, but archaeologists are getting closer to uncovering some clues.

Some of the statues tower 33 FEET (10 m) tall and weigh up to 80 TONS (72 t).

The island is now considered part of CHILE—even though it's 2,200 MILES (3,540 km) off the coast.

The statues were CARVED between A.D. 1200 and 1500.

They are made out of TUFF—a rock created by VOLCANIC ASH that is soft and easy to carve.

Easter Island spans 63 SQUARE MILES (163 sq km).

One theory says the volcanic rock was NUTRIENT-RICH, and the moai could have been scattered across the island to help CROPS GROW.

The island is the MOST ISOLATED landmass on Earth.

The now barren island was once covered in tons of PALM TREES.

A manuscript called Rongorongo, written on WOODEN TABLETS, was discovered on the island in the 19th century, but no one has been able to decipher its meaning.

Amelia Earhart with plane

The
MYSTERY
of AMELIA
EARHART

On July 2, 1937, **Amelia Earhart** steered her plane above the Pacific Ocean. She was **attempting to fly around the world.** Earhart had already covered 20,000 miles (32,187 km), **making several pit stops.** Now she was set to fly 2,556 miles (4,113 km) from New Guinea to Howland Island. But during this flight, Earhart **lost radio contact—and vanished.**

What happened? For decades, people have tried to find out.

Amelia Earhart and Fred Noonan planning their flight route

BORN TO FLY

Amelia Earhart grew up in the midwestern United States. As a young adult, she saw an air show in California. She knew then that she wanted to learn to fly. After taking lessons, Earhart earned her pilot's license. She went on to become the first woman to fly solo across the Atlantic. She also set at least four other world aviation records. In 1937, the now famous pilot decided to fly around the world. Earhart and her navigator, Fred Noonan, took off on June 1 from Miami, Florida, U.S.A. About 40 days later, they disappeared.

After Earhart and Noonan lost contact over the Pacific Ocean, President Franklin D. Roosevelt sent nine ships and 66 aircraft to find them. The rescuers searched for weeks. But the fliers and their plane had vanished. Since then, scientists have been trying to piece together what might have occurred.

FINDING AMELIA

Researchers have a few theories about Amelia Earhart's final flight. The most common one is that Earhart's plane ran out of fuel and crashed near Howland Island. Afterward, the plane sank deep into the Pacific Ocean.

Another theory is that the plane landed on a coral reef south of Howland. In the days after the flight's disappearance, radio signals were sent from a small island next to the reef. These could have been distress calls from Earhart and Noonan. There are also reports of human bones found on the island by British explorers in 1940. Researchers who've studied the island haven't come across debris from a plane. But they think it's possible the plane floated away sometime after landing—and its passengers then perished on the island.

YOU NEVER KNOW

Despite these theories, no one can prove just yet what happened to Amelia Earhart. Scientists will continue looking for clues about her fate. But we may never find out the whole truth. One thing is for sure: Amelia Earhart's adventurous spirit has inspired generations of people. And this pilot's life, and the puzzles she left behind, can still our make our imaginations fly.

AMELIA EARHART HAD A BRIGHT YELLOW PLANE SHE NAMED THE CANARY.

Amelia Earhart with crowd after second Atlantic crossing

WHEN EARHART RECEIVED HER PILOT'S LICENSE IN 1923, SHE WAS ONLY THE 16TH WOMAN IN THE UNITED STATES TO DO SO.

DURING HER SOLO FLIGHT ACROSS THE ATLANTIC OCEAN, AMELIA ENJOYED A CUP OF HOT CHOCOLATE.

Which Wonder **WOULD YOU CHOOSE?**
NASCA LINES vs.
WHITE HORSE HILL

If you were an archaeologist called to solve one of the world's biggest mysteries, which riddle would you rather decode?

NASCA LINES
Where: Peru

Are aliens trying to communicate with us? That's what some believe is the purpose of more than 1,000 designs of shapes, animals, plants, humans, and gods that were carved into the ground some 2,000 years ago. This is extraterrestrial excitement at its best, but researchers are confident these lines were created by the Nasca people, who lived in what is present-day Peru. But what's the purpose of this ancient artwork? One theory suggests the lines represent groups of stars or a calendar, while another supposes that they were created to guide spiritual rituals—people may have danced on the lines as part of these ceremonies in hopes of bringing rain during a drought.

There are more than 800 straight lines, some of which stretch for 30 miles (48 km).

This area of Peru is one of the driest places on Earth, so the lack of rain and erosion has kept the lines intact for centuries.

The ancient images span nearly 170 miles (270 km).

The Nasca people had no written language, which gave great importance to images.

Some images are 1,200 feet (366 m) long and are best viewed from above.

During World War II, the giant carving was covered with grass and trimmings so that enemy aircraft bombers couldn't use it to help navigate the area.

England has 56 hill figures, but the Uffington horse is the oldest.

The horse is visible from 20 miles (32 km) away.

There is an annual "chalking day," in which anyone can join in on the upkeep of the horse carving.

If people didn't continually manicure the horse, it would have disappeared within 20 to 30 years.

UFFINGTON WHITE HORSE
Where: Oxfordshire, England, U.K.

A giant horse the length of a football field carved into a chalky hillside has mystified people for 3,000 years. The world is dying to know who built it and why, but the truth still remains hidden. Could it represent Fhiannon, the golden-clad horse goddess of Welsh mythology? Or does it instead honor ancient myths that often showed a horse pulling the chariot of the sun? Or what if it's not a horse at all, but a dragon? In one story, St. George slayed a dragon, whose blood spilled down the hill, leaving a white chalk scar where no grass will ever grow.

Fingerprints:
CRACKING
THE CASE

No one knows for sure why we have fingerprints.

One theory suggests that fingerprints help our sense of touch, communicating more sensitive information to our brain.

SKIN IS THE HUMAN BODY'S LARGEST ORGAN, AND MUCH OF IT IS STILL A MYSTERY.

SO WHAT'S THE SKINNY ON WHAT WE DO KNOW?

Our skin tells us a lot about what's happening both inside and outside of our body. When a cool breeze passes by, we get goose bumps, which is our body's attempt to keep us warm. On a sunny day our palms don't tan as much as the rest of our body because the skin is thicker there, they're less fragile, and they have less exposure to the sun. Comparing our palms to the rest of our skin, we can see if we've gotten a little too much sun!

But there are some pieces to the skin puzzle that we can't quite connect. Take, for instance, blushing. When we are embarrassed, a surge of adrenaline pumps blood a little faster through our vessels. Our cheeks are wired with veins. For some reason, when something uncomfortable happens, the veins in our cheeks open up, allowing more blood to flow through, saucing our cheeks like a bowl of spaghetti.

SUPER **SKIN-TERESTING!**

Another theory suggests fingerprints provide an extra layer of protection.

Originally, fingerprints were thought to help human grip, but they could actually worsen it.

Adermatoglyphia is a rare condition in which someone is born without fingerprints.

Mysterious MUMMIES

MUMMIES HAVE BEEN FOUND ALL OVER THE WORLD, from Chile to Egypt to Russia. Some were deliberately preserved, like ancient Egyptian pharaohs who were wrapped in fabric and placed in tombs. Others were mummified by accident after being trapped under ice or in bogs. But all mummies carry with them secrets of the past. Discover incredible stats about these puzzling time travelers.

Ötzi, an ancient mummy discovered in a glacier in Europe, has **61 tattoos.**

Found in Chile, the oldest deliberately preserved mummies were made **7,000 years ago.**

Medieval mummies in northern Russia were buried with bronze bowls from **3,700 miles (6,000 km)** away in southwestern Asia.

Hunters came upon a group of 8 **500-year-old mummies** in Greenland buried with **78 pieces of clothing.**

Experts **spent 10 months** designing a lifelike model of the face of a mummy from Peru.

A **60,000-pound (27,216-kg)** sarcophagus with **3 mummies** was uncovered in Alexandria, Egypt.

More than **100 Inca mummies** have been found with silver and gold figurines high in South America's Andes Mountains.

In ancient Egypt, a mummy's lungs, liver, intestines, and stomach were put in **4 separate jars.**

Ancient Egyptian mummies were wrapped in about **450 feet (137 m) of fabric—** that's longer than a football field!

Researchers re-created the sound of a **3,000-year-old mummy's voice** using a **3D model** of his vocal cords!

The British Museum exhibits a **12-foot (3.7-m)-long mummified crocodile** from ancient Egypt.

One mummy unearthed in China had **4,000-year-old pieces of cheese** around her neck.

The ancient Egyptians' mummification process took **70 days.**

Cryptic CREATURES

These RARE ANIMALS have MIND-BLOWING BEHAVIORS.

SNOW LEOPARD

It may seem impossible for any creature to survive high up in the snowy mountains. But the snow leopard was made to combat this chilly habitat 24/7. With a white fur coat speckled with dark gray spots, this big cat is practically invisible against the frozen backdrop as it hunts. Its paws are cushioned with thick pads that protect its feet from the harsh cold and sharp, craggy mountainsides. If perched on a windy peak, the cat wraps its long, fluffy tail around its body for extra warmth.

PANGOLIN

With scales strong enough to withstand a lion's bite, pangolins are a force to be reckoned with. When they sense a predator, they curl up into a ball to protect themselves, letting their scales send a "stay back" message while they slash their spiky tail through the air like a sword. But even a sturdy suit of armor can't protect pangolins from being one of the most illegally trafficked animals in the world. They're poached for their scales, which are used in traditional medicines, and for their meat. Conservation groups work to educate the public and to fund research to learn more about this magnificent mammal.

Baby pangolins ride on their mother's tail so that if threatened, they can slip under her as she rolls into a ball to protect them.

FOREST ELEPHANT

These gentle giants are saving the rainforest, and it's all thanks to their love of fruit! Forest elephants spend 70 to 90 percent of their day foraging for food, scattering seeds while they merrily munch. Along the way, they use their tusks to dig through the dirt, which helps loosen the soil and mix up minerals that help plants grow. But one more ingredient helps the forest as the elephants feast—poop! Elephant droppings are a natural fertilizer, helping sprout new trees and keeping the environment in perfect balance.

GREENLAND SHARK

This sleek submarine of a shark is full of surprises—nothing holds it back from finding a yummy meal. Though it might swim only 0.6 mile an hour (1 km/h), don't let its sloth-like pace fool you. When it senses food, it releases a sudden burst of energy to quickly snag its prey. It even withstands the frigid Arctic waters year-round, swimming as deep as 7,200 feet (2,200 m) to feast on the cryptic creatures that live in the ocean's darkest depths. Slow and steady wins the race, because this shark can live to be 400 years old, making it the longest-living known vertebrate on the planet.

Most Greenland sharks are blind due to a parasite that lives in their eyes.

ALIENS:
ARE THEY OUT THERE?

Imagine standing in the middle of a dark field. **Bright lights suddenly appear** directly above you, but it's not clear who—or what—could be waiting on **the other side.** Maybe it's a **green blob** with **three eyes,** a **robot** made of **all-knowing alien technology,** or maybe llamas have been aliens in disguise all along! One thing's for sure, some things just **can't be explained ...** yet.

FIRE OPALS FOUND ON A METEORITE FROM MARS COULD HELP IN THE HUNT FOR LIFE ON THE RED PLANET.

ALIENS WELCOME

In 1994, scientists thought fragments of a comet were going to hit Jupiter. Unsure of how big of an impact it would have, the people of Wyoming, U.S.A., dubbed a 5,000-foot (1,520-m) landing strip the Greater Green River Intergalactic Spaceport, ready to welcome any aliens from Jupiter that would need to seek refuge on Earth. Nothing ever landed (as far as we know), but the landing strip is still there today.

UFO SIGHTINGS

Though the existence of aliens is easy to dismiss, how do we respond when trusted sources share stories of personal encounters? Between 2017 and 2018, military footage was released of what the U.S. Navy confirmed to be "unidentified aerial phe-nomena"—aka UFOs. And multiple astronauts have claimed to see UFOs while in space. For about 20 years, the U.S. government led Project Blue Book, which investigated 12,618 UFO sightings; 701 of those sightings remain unidentified today.

NEW CREATURES

In the Milky Way alone—one of billions of galaxies in the universe—are several hundred billion stars, and scientists think that every one of those stars has at least one planet orbiting it. This makes the odds of finding life pretty high, but it might not be the aliens that we see in movies—it could likely be as small as the microbial life on our own planet. Scientists study Earth's most extreme environments to understand how the rarest of life can exist elsewhere in our solar system.

In particular, scientists are excited about a moon that has the potential to hold life. Europa—one of Jupiter's 79 moons—has an outer shell of ice. Scientists suspect there is a large ocean under-neath that has three times the volume of liquid water found in all of the oceans on Earth. Perhaps a school of new creatures are swimming there. But because sunlight can't get through the thick top layer of ice, what lies beneath is still a mystery—though hopefully not for long!

View of Milky Way galaxy from Zion National Park, Utah, U.S.A.

Europa, one of Jupiter's moons

YOU CAN VISIT AN ALIEN WATCHTOWER IN HOOPER, COLORADO, U.S.A.

IN CELEBRATION OF A LOCAL 1986 UFO SIGHT-ING, CAPILLA DEL MONTE, CORDOBA, ARGENTINA, HAS AN ANNUAL INTERNATIONAL ALIEN FESTIVAL WITH THOU-SANDS OF ATTENDEES.

INDEX

CREDITS

AL=Alamy Stock Photo; AS=Adobe Stock; GI=Getty Images; NGIC=National Geographic Image Collection; SS=Shutterstock

FRONT COVER: (background circles throughout), Helen st/SS; (golden sparkle throughout), Thanakorn/AS; (satellite), NASA; (Shwedagon Pagoda), martinhosmat083/AS; (vase), Purchase, 1896/Metropolitan Museum of Art; (pufferfish), Judex/AS; (dinosaur), Franco Tempesta; (robe), Gift of Mr. and Mrs. George F. Miller, 1970/Metropolitan Museum of Art; (Stonehenge), vencav/AS; (aurora borealis), Pi-Lens/SS; (spider), Jürgen Otto; (sifaka), Jurgen and Christine Sohns/FLPA/Minden Pictures; **SPINE:** (seahorse), Alex Mustard/Nature Picture Library; (King Tut), Ivan Soto Cobos/SS; (surgeonfish), DeAgostini/GI; (robe), Gift of Mr. and Mrs. George F. Miller, 1970/Metropolitan Museum of Art; **BACK COVER:** (bear), Ian McAllister/NGIC; ("Pillars of Creation"), NASA and the Hubble Heritage Team (STSCI/AURA)/NGIC; (lily pads), Svetlana Chekhlova/AS; (Himeji Castle), Sean Pavone/AS; **FRONT MATTER:** 1, Alex Mustard/Nature Picture Library; 2 (UP LE), Jurgen and Christine Sohns/FLPA/Minden Pictures; 2 (UP RT), naka00/SS; 2 (LO LE), Eravong Komalamena/EyeEm/AS; 2 (LO RT), Gift of Mr. and Mrs. George F. Miller, 1970/Metropolitan Museum of Art; 3 (UP), Judex/AS; 3 (LO LE), Siraphob Werakijpanich/SS; 3 (LO RT), Realy Easy Star/AL; 4 (UP), bbsferrari/AS; 4 (LO), Paul Nicklen/NGIC; 5 (LE), Horst Ossinger/picture-alliance/dpa/AP Photo; 5 (RT), Look and Learn/Bridgeman Images; 6 (UP), A.N.T./Science Source; 6 (LO), Janos/AS; 7 (UP), Andrey Armyagov/SS; 7 (LO), Pavlinec/Dreamstime; **CHAPTER 1:** 8-9, May_Lana/SS; 10 (LE), Matthew/AS; 10 (RT), superjoseph/AS; 11 (UP), Elizabeth/AS; 11 (LO), Vlad61/SS; 12 (UP), Andrii Vergeles/AS; 12 (LO), Lucille/AS; 13 (UP), Josemaria Toscano/AS; 13 (LO), NatureStock/AS; 14-15, JekLi/SS; 14 (LE), Federico Franzone/AS; 14 (RT), robertharding/AL; 15 (LE), Science History Images/AL; 15 (CTR), aorlyan/AS; 15 (RT), JKeiser/AS; 16 (LE), Grant Dixon/Minden Pictures; 16 (RT), T photography/SS; 17 (UP LE), Borge Ousland/NGIC; 17 (UP RT), John Barger/Danita Delimont/AS; 17 (LO LE), ggfoto/AS; 17 (LO RT), Dinodia Photos/AL; 18-19, Tanaonte/GI; 20 (UP), Sarit Richerson/SS; 20 (LO LE), Holmes Garden Photos/AL; 20 (LO RT), panurut/AS; 21 (LE), mickey_41/AS; 21 (UP), Anne/AS; 21 (CTR), DK Media/AS; 21 (LO), Svetlana Chekhlova/AS; 22 (UP LE), Uwe Moser/AS; 22 (UP RT), Weiquan Lin/Moment RF/GI; 22 (LO), Inge Johnsson/AL; 23 (UP LE), Nina B/SS; 23 (UP RT), surangaw/AS; 23 (LO LE), Douglas Peebles Photography/AL; 23 (LO RT), Hemis/AL; 24, Carsten Peter/NGIC; 25 (UP), Martin Edstrom/NGIC; 25 (RT), emperorcosar/SS; 25 (LO), Dennis Dela Cuesta Murillo/AL; 26-27, John Finney photography/GI; 28-29 (UP), Janos/AS; 28 (RT), PhotoElite/AS; 28 (LO), Kent Kobersteen/NGIC; 29 (UP), Vito Fusco/GI; 29 (LO LE), Ibrahim Faiz/EyeEm/GI; 29 (LO RT), WanRu Chen/GI; 30, Volosh/AS; 31, Sven Taubert/AS; **CHAPTER 2:** 32-33, Frans Lanting/NGIC; 34-35, Shahar Shabtai/SS; 36, warpaintcobra/AS; 37 (UP), Sergey Krasovskiy/Stocktrek Images/GI; 37 (RT), (LO), Franco Tempesta; 38-39, Paul Nicklen/NGIC; 38, A.N.T./Science Source; 39 (LE), damedias/AS; 39 (RT), Jeannette Katzir/SS; 40 (LE), Agnieszka Bacal/SS; 40 (RT), Andrey Gudkov/Dreamstime; 41 (LE), Stephen Dalton/Avalon/AL; 41 (UP), Ivan Histand/SS; 41 (CTR), John Cancalosi/AL; 41 (LO LE), Irina K./AS; 41 (LO RT), AardLumens/AS; 42 (UP LE), Solvin Zankl/Nature Picture Library; 42 (UP RT), Daniela Dirscherl/WaterFrame/AGE Fotostock; 42 (LO), Fabien Michenet/Minden Pictures; 43 (UP LE), Philippe Garcelon; 43 (UP RT), Denis Crawford/AL; 43 (LO LE), Eye of Science/Science Source; 43 (RT), McPhoto/Weber/AL; 44-45, Donald M. Jones/Minden Pictures; 44, Martin Harvey/GI; 45, Cigdem Sean Cooper/SS; 46-47, WaterFrame/AL; 48-49, Jürgen Otto; 48 (CTR), Sumukha J.N.; 48 (RT), Thyrymn2/SS; 49 (LE), mrfiza/SS; 49 (RT), Rafaela Asprino/SS; 50 (UP LE), Oleksiy Mark/SS; 50 (UP RT), Rebecca Cave/AL; 50 (LO), Frans Lanting/NGIC; 51 (UP LE), George Grall/AL; 51 (UP RT), geraldmarella/AS; 51 (LO LE), Simon Booth/SS; 51 (LO RT), Impala/AS; 52-53, Roger de la Harpe/SS; 54, Robert Clark/NGIC; 55 (UP), Prof. Mark Cutkosky; 55 (LO), nico99/AS; **CHAPTER 3:** 56-57, happystock/AS; 58 (UP), sculpies/AS; 58 (LO), 59 (UP), (LO), Archives Charmet/Bridgeman Images; 60 (UP), AGE Fotostock/AL; 60 (LE), ART Collection/AL; 60 (LO), DeAgostini/GI; 61 (1), Yuri Yavnik/SS; 61 (2), RuthChoi/SS; 61 (3), Waj/SS; 61 (4), Viacheslav Lopatin/SS; 61 (5), Mark Schwettmann/SS; 61 (6), Victor Torres/SS; 61 (7), Dan Breckwoldt/SS; 62-63, David Santiago Garcia/Westend61/AL; 63 (UP), liskam/AS; 63 (LO CTR), A.Jedynak/AS; 63 (LO RT), jiawangkun/AS; 64 (UP LE), Historical Views/AGE Fotostock/AL; 64 (UP RT), Lmarc1/Dreamstime; 64 (LO), Funkystock/AGE Fotostock; 65 (UP LE), Jesús de Fuensanta/AS; 65 (UP), Purchase, Edward S. Harkness Gift, 1926/Metropolitan Museum of Art; 65 (LO LE), Purchase, 1896/Metropolitan Museum of Art; 65 (LO RT), Gift of Mr. and Mrs. George F. Miller, 1970/Metropolitan Museum of Art; 66, Stockbym/AS; 67 (UP), Mondolithic Studios; 67 (LO), Mondolithic Studios; 67 (CTR), Universal History Archive/UIG/SS; 68-69, Mazur Travel/AS; 68, Tiago Fernandez/AS; 69 (LE), photoaliona/AS; 69 (RT), naka00/SS; 70 (LE), esvetleishaya/AS; 70 (RT), Oksana Perkins/AS; 71 (UP LE), Animaflora PicsStock/AS; 71 (UP CTR), Shawn Hempel/AL; 71 (UP RT), Nicola Forenza/AS; 71 (CTR), imageBROKER/SS; 71 (LO LE), lexan/AS; 71 (LO RT), Prism6 Production/AS; 72-73, Mapics/SS; 74, bbsferrari/AS; 75, lkunl/AS; 76, Stephen Chung/AL; 77 (UP LE), John Keates/AL; 77 (UP RT), Jaroslav Moravcik/SS; 77 (LO LE), Art Media/Heritage Images/The Print Collector/AL; 77 (LO RT), Realy Easy Star/AL; 78-79, Karol Kozłowski/AS; 78, Wil.Amaya/AS; 79 (LE), Juergen Ritterbach/AL; 79 (CTR), Wil.Amaya/AS; 79 (RT), jkraft5/AS; **CHAPTER 4:** 80-81, NASA; 82 (UP), Suronin/Dreamstime; 82 (LO), Jaime Jacott/SS; 83 (UP), efired/AS; 83 (CTR), Matt Cowan/Sweden-Treehotel/Reuters; 83 (LO), Airpano Llc/ZUMA Press/Newscom; 84 (UP), sarlay/AS; 84 (CTR), P umatti Sergio/Prisma by Dukas Presseagentur GmbH/AL; 84 (LO), Pavlinec/Dreamstime; 85 (UP), Ian Dagnall/AL; 85 (LO), Wandycz Kasia/GI; 86-87, PitK/AL; 88-89, Sean Pavone/Dreamstime; 88 (CTR), Chee-Onn Leong/AS; 88 (RT), Benny Marty/AL; 89 (LE), Sean Pavone/AS; 89 (RT), Nikada/GI; 90 (UP), Kunal Khurana/AS; 90 (LO LE), Dmitry Orlov/Dreamstime; 90 (LO RT), Richard Clark/GI; 91 (UP LE), Kate Rubins/NASA; 91 (UP RT), Rafael Ben-Ari/AS; 91 (LO LE), Dubai Miracle Garden; 91 (LO RT), Design Pics Inc/AL; 92-93, NASA; 92, elroce/AS; 93 (RT), (LO RT), NASA; 93 (LO LE), GSFC/NASA; 94-95, Moonie's World/AL; 94 (LO LE), Pawel Kopczynski/Reuters; 94 (LO), sabrinaphototraveladdict/SS; 95 (UP RT), Melinda Nagy/AS; 95 (LO LE), Mart_G/GI; 95 (LO RT), oliverfoerschner/SS; 96 (UP LE), Mike Browne/SS; 96 (UP RT), EyesTravelling/AS; 96 (LO), Dmytro Surkov/SS; 97 (UP LE), millaf/AS; 97 (RT), Jarmo V/AS; 97 (LE), Jon Arnold Images Ltd/AL; 97 (LO RT), Mirko Kuzmanovic/SS; 98, Ritu Manoj Jethani/SS; 99 (UP), refrina/AS; 99 (LO), Mauricio Collado/Xinhua/AL; 100-101, Jim West/AL; 100, Joseph Sohm/SS; 101 (LE), Yonhap News/YNA/Newscom; 101 (RT), NASA; 102, Maarten Reeders/CuliAir Skydiving; 103, Abrar Sharif/SS; **CHAPTER 5:** 104-105, John Chumack/Science Source; 106-107, Ron Miller; 106 (LE), GSFC/S. Wiessinger/NASA; 106 (RT), Lynette Cook/Science Source; 107 (LE), ESO/M. Kornmesser/NASA; 107 (RT), G. Bacon (STScI)/NASA; 108 (UP LE), JPL-Caltech/NASA; 108 (UP RT), GSFC/Solar Dynamics Observatory/NASA; 108 (LO), NASA Image Collection/AL; 109 (UP LE), Stocktrek Images/AL; 109 (UP RT), JPL-Caltech/NASA; 109 (LO LE), NASA/NGIC; 109 (LO RT), Science History Images/AL; 110-111, NASA/AL; 112 (UP), NASA; 112 (LO LE), Jason Reed/Reuters/AL; 112 (LO RT), John White Photos/AL; 113 (LE), Wu Hong/EPA/SS; 113 (UP), Andrew Waddington/Solent News/SS; 113 (CTR), JPL-Caltech/Space Science Institute/NASA; 113 (LO), Yury/AS; 114, Handout/GI; 115 (UP), NASA and the Hubble Heritage Team (STSCI/AURA)/NGIC; 115 (LE), GSFC/NASA; 115 (RT), GSFC/DOE/Fermi LAT/D. Finkbeiner et al./NASA; 116-117, allexxandarx/AS; 116 (CTR), 3d vicka/AS; 116 (RT), blueringmedia/AS; 117 (LE), blueringmedia/AS; 117 (RT), Stocktrek Images/AL; 118 (UP), Björn Wylezich/AS; 118 (LO LE), NASA; 118 (LO RT), NASA, ESA, and M. Livio and the Hubble 20th Anniversary Team (STScI); 119 (UP LE), Oleg Znamenskiy/AS; 119 (UP RT), STS-125 Crew/NASA; 119 (LO LE), NASA; 119 (LO RT), Johns Hopkins University Applied Physics Laboratory/Southwest Research Institute/NASA; 120-121, JPL-Caltech/MSSS/NASA; 122-123, David Aguilar; 122 (CTR), Joel Kowsky/NASA; 122 (RT), designua/AS; 123 (LE), weyo/AS; 123 (RT), Janez Volmajer/AS; 124, SpaceX/AL; 125 (UP), SpaceX/ZUMA Wire/ZUMA Press/Newscom; 125 (LO LE), Paopano/AS; 125 (LO RT), Richard Carson/Reuters; **CHAPTER 6:** 126-127, Posnov/GI; 128-129, marksn.media/AS; 128 (LE), Prof. Jörg Wiedenmann; 128 (LO), Mai/AS; 129 (RT), Arne Hodalic/GI; 129 (LO), Juan Carlos Munoz/AS; 130 (UP), Ievgen Skrypko/AS; 130 (LE), robertharding/AS; 130 (LO), Joseph Khoury/AL; 131 (UP), JFL Photography/AS; 131 (LE), Lauren Dauphin/NASA Earth Observatory; 131 (LO), Airpano Llc/ZUMA Press/Newscom; 132, CrackerClips Stock Media/SS; 133 (UP), Rixie/AS; 133 (CTR), Shchipkova Elena/SS; 133 (LO), Marc Henauer/Solent News/SS; 134 (UP LE), FLPA/Steve Trewhella/SS; 134 (UP RT), Paul Starosta/GI; 134 (LO), imageBROKER/Media Bakery; 135 (UP LE), Douglas Klug/GI; 135 (UP RT), Konstantin Novikov/SS; 135 (LO LE), David Shale/Nature Picture Library; 135 (LO RT), Roberto Nistri/AL; 136 (CTR), hakbak/AS; 136 (LO), ftlaudgirl/AS; 137 (UP LE), Awashima Marine Park/GI; 137 (UP RT), Andrea Izzotti/AS; 137 (CTR), Paulo de Oliveira/Photoshot/AGE Fotostock; 137 (LO LE), Wildestanimal/AS; 137 (LO RT), Andy Murch/ImageQuestMarine; 138-139, Charles Nicklin/NGIC; 138, David Doubilet/NGIC; 140, Nature Picture Library/AL; 141, Zaid Saadallah/Dreamstime; 142-143, Martin Vlnas/SS; 142, Dudarev Mikhail/AS; 143 (LE), kovop58/AS; 143 (RT), Robert Hiette/SS; 144-145, BIOSPHOTO/AL; 145 (UP), Daniel Huebner/SS; 145 (RT), John Carnemolla/SS; 145 (LO), Frantisek Hojdysz/AS; 145 (LO RT), D. Kucharski K. Kucharska/SS; 146 (UP LE), World History Archive/AL; 146 (UP RT), Darlyne Murawski/NGIC; 146 (LO), Michael Melford/NGIC; 147 (LE), Norbert Wu/Minden Pictures; 147 (UP RT), Stewart Kirk/SS; 147 (LO LE), Sharon Talson/AL; 147 (RT), David/AS; 148-149, Sergey Novikov/AS; 148, Patricio Robles Gil/Nature Picture Library; 149 (LO CTR), Reinhard Dirscherl/AL; 149 (LO), Claudio Contreras/Nature Picture Library; **CHAPTER 7:** 150-151, Kevin Ebi/Living Wilderness; 152-153, Erlend Haarberg/Nature Picture Library; 152 (CTR), Westend61/AS; 152 (RT), lukakikina/AS; 153 (LE), Matyas Rehak/AL; 153 (RT), Markus/AS; 154 (LE), Berkehaus/Dreamstime; 154 (RT), Chia Chuin Wong/SS; 155 (UP), giedriius/AS; 155 (LE), Norbert Probst/imageBROKER/SS; 155 (RT), Valt Ahyppo/SS; 156, Thomas Barwick/GI; 157 (UP), Felix Mizioznikov/AS; 157 (RT), Brittany Cockrum/SS; 157 (LO), Robert Markowitz/GI; 158-159, Westend61/AS; 159 (UP), Anky10/Dreamstime; 159 (CTR), kurt_G/SS; 159 (LO RT), G.J. Verspui/SS; 159 (LO), Justin Hofman/AL; 160 (UP), Art Wolfe/GI; 160 (LO LE), khunta/AS; 160 (RT), Nature and Science/AL; 161 (UP), Skip Brown/NGIC; 161 (UP RT), Francois Gohier/Science Source; 161 (LO LE), Hap/Quirky China News/SS; 161 (RT), Babak Tafreshi/NGIC; 162-163, Susannah Ireland/SS; 164 (LE), Holmes Coastal Images/AL; 164 (CTR), Feng Xu/GI; 165 (UP), Frankris/SS; 165 (RT), mrallen/AS; 165 (LO), De Visu/AS; 166-167, Joel Sartore, National Geographic Photo Ark/NGIC; 166 (CTR), nopporn/AS; 166 (RT), Vladislav Klimin/SS; 167 (LE), Martin Prochazkacz/SS; 167 (CTR), slowmotiongli/AS; 167 (RT), Anjark/AS; 168 (LE), Cyril Ruoso/Nature Picture Library; 168 (RT), KPixMining/AS; 168 (LO RT), Clarence Holmes Wildlife/AL; 169 (UP), Vincent Yu/AP Photo; 169 (CTR), Dan Ross/AS; 169 (LO LE), Kevin Ebi/Living Wilderness; 169 (LO RT), Jerry Lodriguss/Science Source; 170 (UP), Dusan Radivojevic/AS; 170 (pule cheese), Marko Djurica/Reuters; 170 (honey), Maridav/AS; 170 (bee on flower), cloud9works/AS; 171 (UP), Cephas Picture Library/AL; 171 (RT), Tomoko A. Hosaka/AP Photo; 171 (LO), Hemis/AL; **CHAPTER 8:** 172-173, Sueddeutsche Zeitung Photo/AL; 175 (UP), Pavel Chagochkin/SS; 175 (LO LE), anibal/AS; 175 (LO RT), Jackal Pan/GI; 176, Aflo/SS; 177 (UP), Thierry Falise/LightRocket/GI; 177 (LO), Teddy Seguin; 178 (UP RT), Wirestock/AS; 178 (LE), Reuters/AL; 178 (LO RT), Splash News/Sea Turtle Inc./Newscom; 179 (UP LE), ZUMA Press/AL; 179 (UP RT), Wolfgang Rattay/Reuters; 179 (CTR), Rick Wilking/Reuters; 179 (LO), Barani Raman; 180-181, Horst Ossinger/picture-alliance/dpa/AP Photo; 180, Tabatha Fireman/GI; 181 (LE), iaremenko/AS; 181 (CTR), Steven Day/AS; 181 (RT), mikkelwilliam/GI; 182-183, Dudarev Mikhail/SS; 182 (UP), (LO RT), Pressfoto/Dreamstime; 183 (UP LE), Jon Nazca/Reuters; 183 (UP RT), Fred Tanneau/GI; 183 (LO), Jon Nazca/Reuters; 184 (UP), imageBROKER/SS; 184 (RT), David Krug/AS; 184 (LO), Zhukova Valentyna/SS; 185 (UP), Per-Anders Pettersson/GI; 185 (LO), Jonathan Nguyen/AL; 186-187 (UP), Marion Kaplan/AL; 186-187 (LO), Ramesh Amruth/imageBROKER/AGE Fotostock; 186, Stefanie/AS; 187 (UP), Mikael Damkier/AS; 187 (LO), MF/AS; 188 (UP LE), Kletr/AS; 188 (UP RT), DmitryDolgikh/AS; 188 (LO LE), Tania Zbrodko/AS; 188 (LO RT), Ritu Maheshwari/EyeEm/GI; 189 (UP LE), Huber & Starke/GI; 189 (UP RT), Sergei Drozd/SS; 189 (LO), David Touchtone/AS; 190-191, Virgin Galactic, LLC; 192, Baykar/Handout/Anadolu Agency/GI; 193, Victor Habbick Visions/Science Source; **CHAPTER 9:** 194-195, robertharding/AL; 196, Stella Sophie/SS; 197 (UP), Andrea Magugliani/AL; 197 (LO), The Walker/AS; 198 (LE), Timofeev Vladimir/SS; 198 (RT), Ingo Bartussek/AS; 199 (UP LE), lindasky76/SS; 199 (UP RT), Matt Gush/SS; 199 (CTR), Science History Images/AL; 199 (LO LE), Gilles Barbier/imageBROKER/SS; 199 (LO RT), DEA/W. Buss/GI; 200 (UP LE), gruberjan/AS; 200 (UP RT), Daniel Eskridge/SS; 200 (LO LE), AlienCat/AS; 200 (LO RT), Science RF/AS; 201 (UP LE), Furiarossa/SS; 201 (UP RT), Look and Learn/Bridgeman Images; 201 (LO), Daniel/AS; 202-203, T Studio/AS; 202 (LE), EcoView/AS; 202 (RT), Paul Nicklen Photography, Inc.; 202 (LO), aphonua/AS; 203 (LE), Daniel/AS; 203 (RT), sidney/AS; 204-205, Volanthevist/GI; 206, Everett Collection/SS; 207 (UP), AP Photo; 207 (RT), Pictorial Press Ltd/AL; 207 (LO), Sueddeutsche Zeitung Photo/AL; 208, Siriwatthana Chankawee/Dreamstime; 209, David Newham/AL; 210-211, DaniloAndjus/GI; 210 (CTR), rohane/AS; 210 (RT), Thomas Barwick/GI; 211 (LE), Farknot Architect/AS; 211 (CTR), Terhox/Dreamstime; 211 (RT), fabioberti.it/AS; 212-213, Enrico Ferorelli; 214 (LE), slowmotiongli/AS; 214 (RT), Peter Titmuss/SS; 215 (UP), gudkovandrey/AS; 215 (LO), Nick Caloyianis/NGIC; 216, danielegay/AS; 217 (RT), Scott/AS; 217 (LO), dottedyeti/AS; **BACK MATTER:** 218, Shchipkova Elena/SS; 219, refrina/AS; 220, NASA/NGIC; 221, Andrea Izzotti/AS; 224, Roberto Nistri/AL

FOR TALIA ROSE —A.S.

Since 1888, the National Geographic Society has funded more than 14,000 research, conservation, education, and storytelling projects around the world. National Geographic Partners distributes a portion of the funds it receives from your purchase to National Geographic Society to support programs including the conservation of animals and their habitats. To learn more, visit natgeo.com/info.

For more information, visit nationalgeographic.com, call 1-877-873-6846, or write to the following address:

National Geographic Partners, LLC
1145 17th Street NW
Washington, DC 20036-4688 U.S.A.

For librarians and teachers: nationalgeographic.com/books/librarians-and-educators

More for kids from National Geographic: natgeokids.com

National Geographic Kids magazine inspires children to explore their world with fun yet educational articles on animals, science, nature, and more. Using fresh storytelling and amazing photography, *Nat Geo Kids* shows kids ages 6 to 14 the fascinating truth about the world—and why they should care. **natgeo.com/subscribe**

For rights or permissions inquiries, please contact National Geographic Books Subsidiary Rights: bookrights@natgeo.com

Designed by Julide Dengel and Fan Works Design

Hardcover ISBN: 978-1-4263-7277-3
Reinforced library binding ISBN: 978-1-4263-7276-6

The publisher would like to thank Kelly Hargrave and Andrea Silen, authors and researchers; Grace Hill Smith, project manager; Avery Naughton, project editor; Lori Epstein, photo manager; Danny Meldung and Steve Rouben, photo editors; Michelle Harris, fact-checker; Alix Inchausti, production editor; and Anne LeongSon and Gus Tello, associate designers.

Printed in South Korea
22/SPSK/1